Picture Piecing

Creating Dramatic Pictorial Quilts

Cynthia England

Acknowledgements

Thanks to the supporting staff who made this book a reality. I am grateful to my students who have taught me so much. Their questions became the basis for this publication.

Thanks to the contributing artists who allowed me to share their beautiful work: Carolyn Allison, Terry Caffrey, Jerryann Corbin, Norma DeHaven, Patty Dillon, Wendy Foist, Rosemary England, Jo Fleming, Rhonda Gabriel, Eunice Hill, Katie Kelly, Libby Lehman, Janice Lippincott, Leigh McDonald, Vicki Mangum, Nan Moore, Kathy Olson, Patricia Pepe, Nancy Pocklington, Beth Prager, Rosie Skowronek, Suzanne Taylor, and Peggy Timmons. Their work is an inspiration.

Special thanks to: Lynn Berna, Gloria Brown, Bob and Jerryann Corbin, Ivy Croft, Patty Dillon, Sharon Dinsmore, Rhonda and David Gabriel, Phyllis Hall, Maryann Jacobsen, Libby Lehman, Jim Morgan, Virginia Spiers, and Joen Wolfrom for their constant encouragement and support.

Much appreciation and love to my husband, Warren, and to my children, Stephen, Travis and Monica, who gave me the freedom to be an artist, a wife and mother simultaneously. Thanks, and love to Ingrid England who is always kind and helpful.

This book is dedicated to my mother, Christine Jahnke, whose contributions to my life and career know no bounds.

Rather than use the Trademark (™) and the Registered Trademark (®) symbols on products referenced throughout this book we have credited them in the Resource Listing. There is no intention of infringement. The product names are used in an editorial context.

England, Cynthia.
    Picture piecing : creating dramatic pictorial quilts / by Cynthia England ; edited by Judi Moretz ; photographer, Don Carico.
        p. cm.
        Includes index.
        LCCN 2002092130
        ISBN 0-9720963-0-2

    1. Patchwork. 2. Quilting. 3. Fabric pictures.
I. Title.

TT835.E54 2002   746.46'0433
                                    QBI02-200540

Credits

Editor-in-Chief..........................Judith Moretz
Technical Editor.......................Judy L. Moyer
Managing Editor...................Jerryann Corbin
Cover Design.................................Peri Poloni
Book Design/Illustration.....Cynthia England
Photography.................................Don Carico

Front Cover Quilt:
   Piece and Quiet by Cynthia England
Back Cover Quilts (top to bottom):
   Open Season by Cynthia England
   Split Rail by Cynthia England
   In the Southern Tradition by Cynthia England
Page 1: Detail, *Land That I Love* by Cynthia England
Page 3: Detail, *Teton Mountains* by Cynthia England

Picture Piecing
Creating Dramatic Pictorial Quilts
©2002 by Cynthia England

England Design
1201 Sunset Drive
Dickinson, TX 77539

www.englanddesign.com

Third Printing
Printed in China

Contents

Note: Photo and Figure numbers match the page numbers on which they appear.

Chapter One

Planning

The biggest drawback in starting a large quilting project is the amount of time the finished piece will take. Many projects never get off the ground because we talk ourselves out of them. Any kind of quilt is a huge time commitment. There aren't many crafts that require such tedious labor and take months and sometimes years to complete.

Reasons for making quilts are changing. No longer is it necessary to make them for winter warmth. Quilts are now made for artistic expression. In a fast-paced society, quilting provides a comforting link to the past, and a tangible basis for time spent in the present. The "I got this much done today" phrase is important to many of us. It is a validation for being here and is a means to leave a piece of ourselves behind.

I find in my own quilt making that I am happiest when I have a variety of projects in progress. I like to have one challenging project; a quilt that has some difficult aspect that stretches my brain. After this time-consuming quilt is finished, I make a tradition-al quilt.

Photo 4 - Detail
Come Into the Light
Cynthia England

Stained glass is a hobby of mine. I loved the way the light was streaming through the leaded glass doors. This quilt took eight months to make and is hand quilted. Full view of the quilt is on Page 6.

Photo 6 - *Come Into the Light*   1992   43" x 64"   Cynthia England
The circles in the woodwork were made from tiny yo-yos turned to the back side. A bias bar was used to make the spindles of wood. The first time I used the Picture Piecing technique was on the black and white tile floor.

Photos 7A and 7B - Details   *Come Into the Light*
Cynthia England
To give the illusion of stained glass (above), white print fabric was reversed and transparent washes of color added. The picture frames on the table (left) were made from fabric printed with ladies' faces. Actual height of the largest picture frame is 1 3/8".
Photographs by C. England.

Traditional piecing is a form of relaxation for me. Quilts are like a puzzle. I know where the pieces go and how to get them there. Quilting is my "cloth psychiatry." I especially enjoy making block exchange quilts. The members of my quilting group pick a traditional block and each woman in the group makes a set of blocks out of one fabric combination. The blocks are traded within the group with the exception of one block which is donated to our quilt guild. It is a great way to make a quilt top for charity. I refer to this as "group therapy."

Therapy benefits aside, quilting has provided me with countless hours of enjoyment, not only from practicing the craft itself, but also from associating with the people involved. Nowhere will you find a better group of friends who will share their talent and time. As I travel to different quilting guilds, I find this experience is universal. If you ever move to another city, join the local quilt guild for immediate acceptance.

I enjoy realism in art. Before I discovered the *Picture Piecing* technique, the only way I knew how to make something look real in quilting was to applique it. I enjoy applique, but it is time-consuming. I can machine stitch much faster than I can hand-stitch. Machine stitching enables me to include more detail. I think these quilts look like applique from a distance.

Techniques outlined in this book are a combination of crafts that I have been involved in over the years. The first time I used the Picture Piecing technique was an accident. I was using a freezer paper method in which the pattern was traced in reverse and then stitched back together.

At the time, I was working on *Come Into the Light* (Photo 6). The quilt top was coming along fine until I came to the black and white tile floor. It was late at night, and I forgot to reverse the pattern. My mistake was fortunate. Instead of working from the back side of the fabric, I was now working from the front. I discovered that if I made a mistake sewing, I could remove the pattern pieces and realign them. My error resulted in devising a great method for viewing my sewing from the front side rather than the back side.

I enjoyed making the tile floor so much that I decided to use the same technique on my next quilt, *Piece and Quiet* (Page 9). I learned ways to organize myself and the tedious process. As with anything, the more experience you have with a particular quilting technique, the better you get at it.

My goal was never to be a pattern designer or quilt teacher. I finished *Piece and Quiet*, and was inundated with questions about the process by which it was made. As a result, I made a pattern to teach at a local quilt shop, and here I am.

I hope you enjoy this technique and the freedom of creativity it offers. Enjoy the journey, listen to your instincts, and GO FOR IT!

Photo 8 - Detail
Piece and Quiet
Cynthia England

A pre-printed fabric with a fox on it was pieced into the water's edge. Many different fabrics were used throughout the quilt: cottons, organza, and upholstery weight fabrics.

Getting Started

Half the battle is making up your mind to *do it!* Most quilters are a traditional bunch and are conservative by nature. You may be afraid of making a mistake or getting stuck at some point. Think of doing one step at a time. Break down the project into little bits, and deal with the problems as they arise. If a mistake is made, you have several options: you can rip it out, applique over it (I refer to applique as damage control), or paint over it. Think of mistakes as "creative opportunities." Many of the quilts in this book had changes made to fix trouble spots. It is the finished product that counts!

In my experience, mistakes generally come out better than anything planned. Challenge yourself and you will be surprised at what you can accomplish. Take a risk. Do not wait until you know all the answers before you begin.

Don't feel as if you must work on only one project at a time. I used to feel guilty if I had several things in progress. You may have learned something from that unfinished project that will help you in the next one. When coming back to an unfinished project, look at it as already half finished, rather than thinking, "I should have finished that already." Having more than one project keeps you from getting bored.

Your Working Space
Get It on the Wall

To make concise drawing and perspective decisions, work on a wall rather than a tabletop. It is impossible to check contrast of fabrics and see perspective if you are looking down on a tabletop. In the studio, I have two design walls. One is for long-term projects, and one is for short-term projects. To make a design wall, go to a building supply store and buy insulation that is sold in 4' x 8' sheets. These come in varying thicknesses. Mine is 1/2" thick and pink in color. I went to the store armed with yellow-headed quilters' pins and systematically checked the different kinds of insulation by going down the aisle, poking them to find out which grabbed the best.

Two sheets of insulation placed side-by-side on the wall make a good large surface. Use small nails to attach them to the wall. Cover with a white piece of flannel, a summer blanket, or a good quality cotton batting by stapling it to the insulation. Use a permanent marker and a quilters' ruler to draw a 2 1/2" grid over the entire surface. Number the grid on the top, side, and down the middle. When transferring a line drawing, this grid proves invaluable. It also works great for squaring up projects and laying out blocks for traditional quilts.

Photo 9 - *Piece and Quiet*   1993   78" x 62"
Cynthia England

This woodland scene began with a 3" x 5" photograph. It took about six months to make and has around 8,000 pieces in it. My children were small at the time, one and a half, three, and six years old. The majority of the quilt was made at night when they were asleep; thus the name *Piece and Quiet*. There are two pre-printed animals in this quilt, a deer and a wolf. They are located near the horizon line. At the time I made this quilt I was frustrated with the daily grind and never ending demands on my time. It became my gauge of what I had accomplished for that day. When it was completed I was thrilled with the result and excited about the technique! Photograph by Ken Wagner.

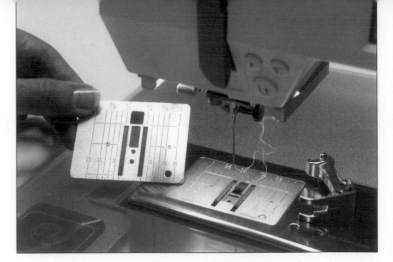

Photo 10A
This photograph illustrates the difference between a single hole needleplate and a standard needleplate. The single hole needleplate (the one with the red sticker on it) works best for small pattern pieces.

The Sewing Space

The Picture Piecing technique requires frequent ironing. Set up two irons. I use a small travel-type iron next to my sewing area on my right side (I am right-handed). This travel iron is used while constructing the sections. I do not recommend the latest tiny irons on a stick (they look like curling irons). They are better suited for applique projects. This technique has small pieces but as you keep working, they get bigger. You will have larger pieced sections to press as you go. I have another regular-sized steam iron I use when joining finished sections. A hard ironing surface works best. It provides an even heat distribution across the entire pattern piece. If the ironing surface is soft, it sinks in where weight is placed. When all of the piecing is completed, I blast the heck out of it with the steam iron.

Lighting

Good lighting is a must! If possible, set your sewing station near natural light. If you are contemplating remodeling your sewing room, I highly suggest florescent lighting and lots of it! Ott lights are very good for close-task lighting. Place one of these right next to your machine. You may want to consider additional electrical outlets as well.

Sewing Machine

This technique only requires a straight line stitch. Students of mine have successfully hand-pieced patterns using this technique. However, hand-piecing causes a problem because the pattern pieces tend to come off with excessive handling. I strongly recommend machine piecing for this technique. It is easy to know where the needle goes in because you can feel the paper.

Any machine that provides a good, even, straight stitch will suffice. A single-hole needleplate is helpful, but not necessary. It has only one hole in which the needle goes up and down (Photo 10A). Zigzagging cannot be done while this plate is on. Featherweights only come with a single-hole needleplate. The advantage of having this needleplate is that

Photo 10B - Use insulation to make a design wall for your sewing room. A gridded design wall is easy to make and is helpful for squaring large quilts. In this photo, the design wall has been covered with a gray sheet for photography purposes.

small pieces of fabric do not get stuck as in the larger zigzag hole.

On my Bernina, I use the #37 patchwork foot. On the Singer Featherweight, I use the foot that originally came on the machine. You do not want a foot that pushes over the fabric because you will be sewing next to a fold. Use a foot that provides good visibility so you can see where the fold is. When facing the machine have the iron on one side and place the master pattern and pattern pieces together on the other side (Photo 22A).

It is important to have the pattern pieces and the master pattern next to each other. Do not tape your pattern to the wall in front of you or place it on the opposite side of the pattern pieces. During construction you will constantly verify placement of the pattern pieces by putting them on top of the Master Pattern. If you place the pattern pieces away from the Master Pattern, it is easy to get pieces out of place or out of sequence.

Helpful Tools

Tracing paper, a roll of freezer paper, a few pencils, transparent tape, drafting tape, a fine lined marker, a straight edge, and a good eraser are all tools you will need for designing (see above). I prefer a colored drafting triangle that you can find in most art supply stores. They are made out of lightweight plastic and do not have any markings on them. You can find them in lime green and neon orange. They come in a variety of sizes

and angle shapes. I have several, but seem to use the 10-inch with a 45-degree angle the most. For designing, I would not recommend using any of the quilters' ruler tools, as the markings on them are distracting. I recommend using a T-square or a carpenter's square for finish work. I use a quilters' ruler, rotary cutter, and mat to square up the completed project.

Tools needed for sewing:

- straight stitch sewing machine
- scissors, to cut fabric and paper
- plastic surface to lay pattern pieces on (such as a sweater or shoebox lid)
- thread to blend with your project (I use a light to medium gray)
- small travel-size iron
- quilters' ruler, mat, and rotary cutter

Tools needed for designing:

- freezer paper
- sharp pencils
- transparent tape
- drafting tape
- fine and medium point permanent markers
- eraser
- clear plastic triangle
- glue stick
- T-square (optional)
- proportional wheel (optional)
- tracing paper (optional)

Chapter Two

Picture Piecing

For years I have been trying to create realistic pictures in cloth. At first, I experimented with applique, traditional piecing and a combination of the two. But, the look I was after was illusive.

After I stumbled onto the Picture Piecing technique I knew that it had definite possibilities. I enjoyed the "puzzle-like" sewing aspects and the freedom from sewing perfect seams. I knew if I was having this much fun, another quilter would too. There is no greater thrill than creating something of your own design.

Over time, I developed notations that helped me during the sewing process. Many of the notations are adaptations from other crafts that I have been involved in. When I came across a specific problem, and I needed a new notation, I made one up.

I like to compare a Picture Pieced pattern to a cross-stitch pattern. They both look incredibly complicated. I understand the pattern notations and they even scare me! But, like a road map, after you learn to read them, the sewing process is actually very simple.

Photo 12 - Detail
In the Southern Tradition
Cynthia England

The azaleas in the original photograph were past their peak, so a gardening book was referenced. Full view of the quilt is on Page 73.

Basic Symbols

In the Picture Piecing technique you will be working with two patterns. One will be a master pattern, the other a freezer paper pattern. The master pattern will be used for reference throughout the sewing process. The freezer paper pattern will be cut apart and used as templates. **Fabric notations** will be identical on the two patterns.

Here are the basic notations:

(1) **Circled numbers** tell where each pattern piece goes after it is cut apart. However, this is not necessarily the order in which the pieces are sewn together. This is one difference from foundation piecing. In foundation piecing, sewing is done *only* in sequential order. With Picture Piecing, *any* two pattern pieces that share a common side can be sewn together. **Circled numbers** denote placement. They give you an idea of what to sew next.

A **Bold lines and letters** indicate major sections. When breaking up a design, the first divisions usually become major sections. After the pattern is divided and notations are placed, these **bold lines** and **bold letters** are the first things that are marked. Major sections are the last seams to be joined. First, sew smaller pattern pieces within the major section together. Then, join the major sections to complete the piece.

■■■ **Dashed lines** help you visualize how the sections must be sewn together and which pattern pieces can be sewn together first. **Dashed lines** are marked on the pattern after all sectioning lines are drawn.

Usually, solid lines are sewn together before **dashed lines**. Visualize a nine-patch block. The three squares must be sewn together before the rows are joined; Picture Piecing uses the same concept. In this technique, you look for two pieces that can be sewn together.

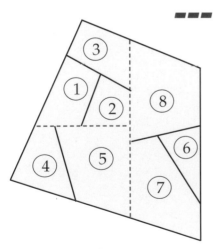

Figure 14A
Dashed lines help visualize smaller sections.

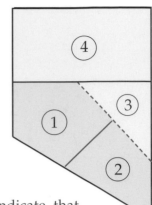

Figure 14B
This **dashed line** tells you to sew pattern pieces 1 and 2 together before you can add pattern pieces 3, then pattern piece 4.

The **dashed lines** indicate that inside the **bold-lined** section there are sub-sections. These must be sewn together first before they can be joined to another group. **Dashed lines** help break up the pattern visually so the smaller sub-sections can be spotted quickly (Figure 14B). **Dashed lines** also indicate which pattern piece is to be sewn on next. In Figure 14C, pattern piece 1 and pattern piece 2 have to be sewn together first before adding 3.

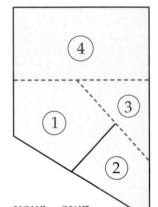

Figure 14C
Another **dashed line** could be placed between pattern pieces 3 and 4 because 3 must be sewn before 4. However, this may look confusing.

When sectioning your own design, be discriminating about how many **dashed lines** you include. If the section is small, there may not be a need for any **dashed lines**. The larger a section is, the more helpful **dashed lines** become. However, too many **dashed lines** can be confusing, rather than helpful. In Figure 14C, another **dashed line** could be placed between pattern pieces 3 and 4 because pattern piece 3 must be sewn on before pattern piece 4. However, the addition of another **dashed line** in this section may look confusing. If only one **dashed line** is added (as in Figure 14B), it provides a better understanding that pattern piece 3 should be sewn before pattern piece 4. If both **dashed lines** are placed on the design, it may appear that pattern piece 4 is sewn on before pattern piece 3. Use of the

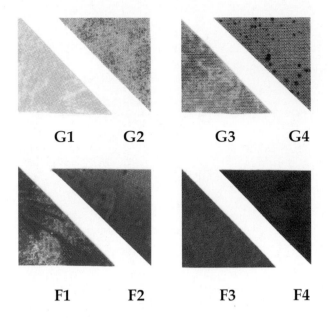

G1 G2 G3 G4

F1   F2   F3   F4

Photo 15A - Make a color chart arranged by shade and value. Under each swatch of fabric write a notation.

dashed line notation is to help visualize which pattern pieces are added in what sequence and to designate smaller sections at a glance.

B, B1

Fabric notations are indicated by small upper-case letters and letters with numbers. These correspond to the fabric selection chart. To make the fabric selection chart, lay out the fabrics by value for each color from light to dark. Clip a small triangle swatch from each fabric. Using a glue stick, attach them to a piece of white paper or card stock (Photo 15A). Under each fabric swatch write a letter notation. For example, if there is only one shade of green, mark the swatch with a G. If there is more than one shade of green, place the fabrics according to value (light to dark). Use the notation G1 for the lightest fabric, G2 for the next darkest, and so on. The higher the number, the darker the fabric. If you are planning to use the front and back of the fabric, cut two swatches and place them according to value.

There are beautiful fabrics which have varying shades in them. If using two or more parts of a single fabric, cut a swatch from

Photo 15B - These fabrics are all directional. Line the arrow in the same direction as the print on the fabric.

each part. Do not expect to remember which part of a fabric you want to use. Time will pass between the designing and sewing, so it would be easy to forget. These notations will tell you which fabric to iron each piece to when they are cut apart.

Arrows are very helpful tools for directional fabrics. They are **not** used for grain line. Use straight **arrows** for straight line fabrics (such as a stripe) and curved **arrows** for fabrics with soft curves (like a paisley). The **arrow** goes in the same direction as the lines (or wavy lines) in your fabric (Photo 15B). If you are piecing a tree and you have this wonderful woodgrain fabric, make sure that the direction of woodgrain goes the way the tree is growing rather than across. **Arrows** on the pattern pieces will tell the direction the woodgrain must go. When using flower fabrics in a landscape quilt, keep in mind which direction the flowers are growing. Flowers grow up rather than sideways.

In foundation piecing, directional fabrics can cause confusion. You have to guess the angle to flip them because you are working on the back side of the fabric. There is no guessing with Picture Piecing. You will be working on the right side of the fabric.

The **arrow** is a notation that grew out of my work with stained glass. In stained glass there are textures which must maintain the same direction throughout the piece.

Photo 16A - *Grandpa's Porch*   2001   26" x 36"
Cynthia England

When I was a child, we lived next door to my grandfather. This wall hanging is reminiscent of the flower bed in the front yard that I played in.

Circle over an intersection indicates that this is an important seam that must match. This is the **only** time a seam must match. For example, if you are piecing a bird and one-half of the bird is in one section and the other half is in another, when joined, the seams must match. Or, when placing the roof on a building, it is important to align the roof precisely over the building. Any discrepancies would be noticeable.

Other Helpful Symbols

The basic symbols are used on all picture pieced patterns; however, you may also find these special symbols helpful:

A **blender arc** was used in the quilt *Grandpa's Porch* (Photo 16A) to designate a fabric that had many variations in it. The fabric went from a light peach to a dark coral. I wanted to make sure that, when the gladiolas were subdivided, I would have the same shade of fabric on each side of the flower division. The **blender arc** was placed over the subdivided line to give me a clue when ironing the pattern pieces onto the fabric (Figure 16B). This notation helps retain fabric continuity throughout the piece.

dk
med
lt

Italic shade notations are helpful to show different values. There are times when you want to place emphasis on a particular object. In the *Snow Scene* pattern (Photo 17A), I wanted the building to stand out. The background around the building was marked with dark notations, using a *dk* symbol to indicate this. In addition, *med* can be used to indicate medium tones of a fabric or *lt*

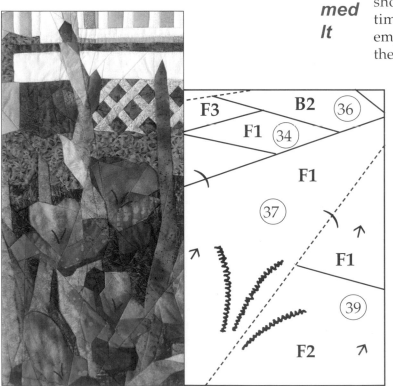

Photo16B - Detail
Grandpa's Porch

Figure 16
The line drawing to the left is a close-up of the flowers on the master pattern of *Grandpa's Porch*. **Blender arc** notations are placed between the sections when the coral fabric crossed over. Be careful to use the same shade of fabric in these areas. The squiggly lines indicate embroidery details.

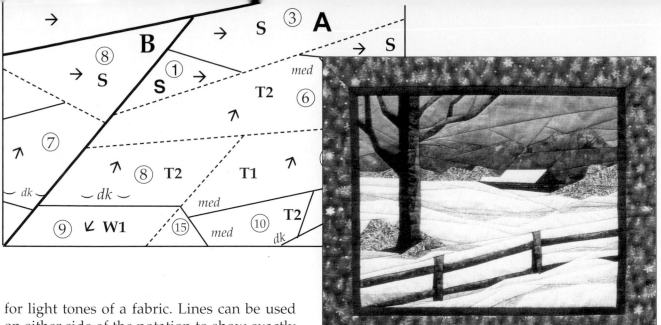

for light tones of a fabric. Lines can be used on either side of the notation to show exactly which area of the pattern piece is to be shaded (Figure 17A). This is very helpful when marking fabrics for flowers, as darks or lights can be placed along the edges of petals to add dimension. The beautiful variations found in fabric available now can create wonderful effects. These notations allow you to use the fabric to its best advantage.

Figure 17A and Photo 17A
Snow Scene　1996　21" x 18"
Cynthia England
Italic shade notations were used in the master pattern around the building to indicate the use of medium and dark fabrics (above right).

● **Solid dots** are helpful to designate overlapping objects. They indicate a visual matching point. Unlike a **circle over an intersection**, two seams do not actually cross over one another, but the seam still must visually align. For example, in *Tropical Scene* (Photo 17B) palm trees in the foreground overlap the water and the mountain range in the background. **Solid dots** used on the pattern indicate these are important places the horizon line must visually line up when the final seams are sewn (Figure 17B). It is best to mark these notations when making the pattern so you can be aware of them as you sew. It is much easier to line up objects in the section stage rather than try to fix an alignment problem after the entire project is sewn.

Photo 17B and Figure 17B
Tropical Scene　2000　19" x 17"
Cynthia England

Solid dots indicate a visual matching point in *Tropical Scene's* (right) master pattern.

Chapter Three

Sewing

If you can sew a straight line, you can master this technique. The basic concept of Picture Piecing is to make the pattern fit the sewing line.

In traditional piecing accuracy is imperative. Measurements must be made carefully, patchwork points must meet, and blocks must measure the exact size. If not, the construction process is a nightmare and the quilt will not lay flat. I enjoy the precision involved in making traditional quilts; however, with the Picture Piecing technique, accuracy is not the top priority.

In traditional piecing, seam allowances are the basis for sewing. In this technique you will be sewing next to a fold, not a precise measurement. As long as the freezer paper pattern pieces meet, the pattern will maintain its size. You will be matching the freezer paper, not the seam allowance. There are only straight lines to sew, no angles, or "set-in" seams.

Through teaching, I have found that the designing process is best understood after the mechanics of the technique are clear. Therefore, I suggest familiarizing yourself with the process by sewing the butterfly test pattern on Page 31 before designing your own pattern.

Photo 18 - Detail
Positano, Italy Coastline

Cynthia England

Some windows were painted and others were pieced. The tiny tourist boat pictured at left is actual size. The full view of quilt is on Page 33. Photograph by Richard Margolis.

Photo 20A - Iron to the right side of fabric.

Photo 20B - Using scissors, cut out leaving approximately 1/4" around.

Prep Work

To begin, place a plastic tray or shoebox lid under your work area and use paper scissors to cut out the **freezer** paper pattern (not the Master Pattern) on the bold lines. Cut out all of the pieces in Section A, place them in a sandwich bag, and label it **Section A**. Each section will be cut out, placed in its own bag, and labeled. You may find a rotary cutter helpful when cutting apart large sections.

Use a cotton setting when ironing the pattern pieces to the fabric. Do not use steam. Work with one section at a time, sorting the pattern pieces by color notation. Press the pattern pieces to the right side of the fabric, leaving 1/4" around each piece (Photo 20A). If there are two pattern pieces of the same color, place them at least 1/2" apart, allowing for a 1/4" seam allowance around each pattern piece. To save time, use the edge of the fabric for one side of the 1/4" seam allowance (Photo 20B).

Take care when cutting seam allowances; cut a generous 1/4". This allows room for repositioning the pattern piece, after sewing, if necessary. Avoid the tendency to cut a proportionally smaller seam allowance on small pattern pieces. Make sure the fabric edges are parallel with the pattern piece edges. Square off and clip any long points to 1/4". The more accurately the pattern pieces are cut, the easier it will be to sew them together. However, there is no need to measure and cut

Photo 20C
Stitch in Time
1997   24" x 20"
Cynthia England

As you can see from the original photograph at the far right. the color scheme was changed on the final wall hanging.

Photo 21A - ⊘ Do not leave uneven edges when cutting out pattern pieces.

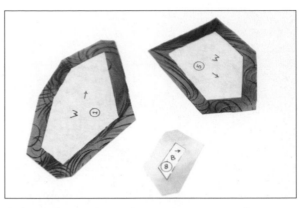

Photo 21B - It is important to keep seam allowances straight and even like the examples above.

them out with a rotary cutter. The first time the pattern pieces are repositioned it will change the perfect seam allowance cut. The important thing to remember is to keep seam lines straight and parallel while you work with them. Trim them constantly while sewing to maintain this straight line.

After ironing on pattern pieces, cut around groups so that they can fit into a zipper-type sandwich bag. Label with the appropriate section. While watching television, I cut out the individual pattern pieces and drop them onto a plastic tray placed in my lap. The pattern pieces are then returned to their labeled section bag. When I begin to sew, the sections are cut and ready to go.

Tip:

When cutting out a new section, first sort the pattern pieces by fabric color. For example, use the plastic tray and pick one corner to stack all background fabrics, another area for all G1 notations, and so on. As the pattern pieces are cut apart, drop them in their color stack. This eliminates resorting the pattern pieces if they are placed in zipper-type sandwich bags. As an alternative to sandwich bags, try stacking shoe box lids on top of each other. They nest neatly into one another.

Photo 21C
Original Photograph
Cynthia England

This photograph was the basis for my wall hanging *Stitch in Time*. I own several Featherweight sewing machines. The one at left is from the early 1940's. The quilt top pictured was purchased at a garage sale for $1.00. Actually, it is half a quilt top. In answer to my question, "Do you have any quilting related items?" the woman having the sale said, "Yes, but I may want to patch some holes on my jeans, so you can have half." To my horror she proceeded to cut the hand pieced quilt top down the middle!

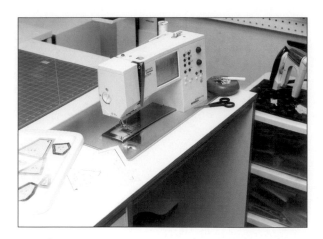

Photo 22A - Place your iron to one side of the sewing machine. On the other, place the pattern pieces and the master pattern near one another. You will be referring to the pattern constantly.

Organizing the Pattern Pieces

There are two ways to organize the pattern pieces. One is by color. You can group pattern pieces by their **color notation**s on a tray; for example, G1's together, G2's, G3's, and so on. Be sure the **circled numbers** can be easily seen.

The second way to organize pattern pieces is by **circled numbers** to determine where the pieces go in the design. Use a sweater box lid to lay out the pattern pieces. A smooth, plastic one works best and allows the pattern pieces to slide around. Look for a lid that has a slightly raised edge (Photo 22B).

Lay out the pattern pieces from one section in the tray. Keep them in a single layer (do not overlap them). It is not necessary to lay them out in exact numeric order, but place them so you can spot the **circled numbers** quickly.

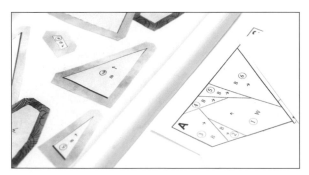

Photo 22B - A plastic lid with a raised edge is helpful. It contains the pattern pieces and they are easily arranged. Blocking off the pattern with white paper or index cards helps to keep your place.

Construction Methods
Sewing Pairs

Locate all pairs within the section and stitch them first. Once these pairs are sewn, continue to add other pattern pieces to make units, and join them to complete the section. Remember to check the placement against the Master Pattern as you go. For example, in Figure 22, pattern pieces 1 and 2, 3 and 4, and 6 and 7 each share a common seam; therefore they are considered pairs. Pattern pieces 4 and 5 could also be considered a pair.

When sewing, use a normal stitch length (12 to 14 stitches per inch) throughout. Unlike foundation piecing (where the stitch length is shortened to allow for paper removal), stitching will be placed next to the freezer paper pattern pieces rather than

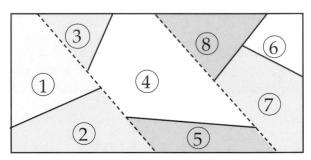

Figure 22 - Locate pairs within a section and begin sewing them first.

through them. **Circled numbers** are used to locate two pattern pieces (a pair). Place the Master Pattern close to the sewing machine, as it will be referred to constantly. During construction, lay the pattern pieces directly on top of the Master Pattern to check placement. Work with only one section at a time. Each section has it's own set of sequential numbers. If more than one section is sewn at a time, there will be duplicate **circled numbers** which will be confusing.

Use 1/4" seams throughout. Sew from end to end without backstitching. When the pattern pieces are sewn together, right sides will face one another (freezer paper to freezer paper). Pull back the corner of the top pattern piece, and make sure the end points of the freezer paper match (Photo 23A). Check

Photo 23A - Match the corners of the freezer paper.

Photo 23B - Pin matched pieces. With the pin, go through the fabric and come up through the paper.

Tip:

Before sewing, determine the pairs within a section. Chain stitch these, iron them and then add to them. Try to work in an assembly-line fashion.

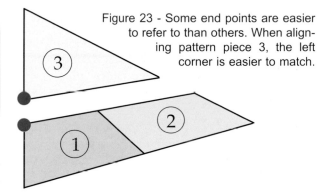

Figure 23 - Some end points are easier to refer to than others. When aligning pattern piece 3, the left corner is easier to match.

only the corners of the pattern pieces. If you look at the whole line, the freezer paper will pop off. When pinning, sometimes it is easier to see one end point of a pattern piece than another (Figure 23). If that is the case, align the side that is the easiest to see. In the illustration, the left side, indicated by the red dot, is easier to line up than the right side. Remember, the seam does not need to be perfect. The pattern piece can be moved.

Pin in the center of the pattern piece, keeping the pin vertical. Pin down through the fabric seam allowance, and come up

through the freezer paper. When placing the pin through the seam allowance, try to insert the pin near the paper edge but not through it (Photo 23B). After the pair is pinned, it will dent slightly away from where the pin goes through and comes up (Photo 23C). Take your fingers and place them on either side of the pin. Fold the fabric back along the edge of the freezer paper (Photo 23D). This fold will be the your sewing guideline. You may find it

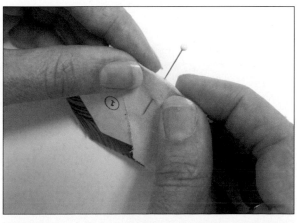

Photo 23C - Use your fingers and fold back, creasing along the freezer paper edges.

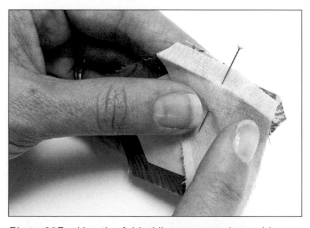

Photo 23D - Use the folded line as a sewing guide.

helpful to use more than one pin for longer pattern pieces. I try to avoid sewing over pins.

Do not agonize about sewing along the fold perfectly. If the fold isn't readily visible, sew a scant 1/4" seam and hope for the best. If the seam allowances were cut close to 1/4", your seam should not be too far off. After sewing the seam, check to see how close the freezer paper pattern pieces are to each other. They must meet along the edges with no fabric showing between the pattern pieces. If they are not aligned, this technique allows

fabrics. You just finished sewing two pattern pieces together, one with flowers the other with grass, and they are too far apart. The pattern pieces can be repositioned exactly on either side of the sewn seam. Or, you have the choice of moving just one pattern piece over the seam to touch the other. This change does not affect the overall look of the design. It doesn't matter if you have a little more flower fabric than grass fabric. The pattern pieces could also be repositioned in the opposite manner, for example, you could have more grass than flower fabric. It is perfectly okay to move the pattern piece over the seam. Just remember that the pattern pieces need to meet after every sewn seam. The pattern will maintain its size if the pattern pieces are aligned. If too much space is allowed between pattern pieces, the next pattern piece to be sewn on will not align.

The only time repositioning a pattern

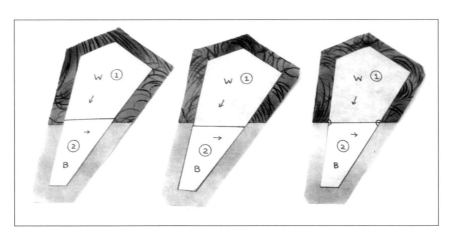

Photo 24 - Pattern pieces can be realigned to either side of the seam. However, do not realign pattern pieces if there is a **circle over an intersection** notation on one of the pattern pieces. In this case, align them exactly on their own color fabric.

alteration of the pattern rather than the fabric.

If there is too much space between the pieces after you have sewn them, remove the freezer paper, reposition the pattern pieces closer to the seam, and iron again (Photo 24). Do not feel guilty when repositioning pattern pieces. This cheating is encouraged! It is better to sew a scant seam and reposition than to sew over the freezer paper. This will not change the outcome of your design because you are not making blocks that must fit together perfectly or where seams must align for the design to look correct.

Here is an example where this may happen. Let's say you are working on a landscape design that contains flower and grass

piece over another color is not a good idea is in the case of a **circle over an intersection** notation. This notation means that there is a color change here that matters. If there is space between the two pattern pieces, you must sew a new seam closer to the pattern to tighten it up. There is no need to remove the stitching already there.

For example, if one half of a flower stem is in one section and the rest is in another section, when the two sections are joined, there will be important seams that must match for the stem to visually align.

I frequently sew the seam a scant 1/4" and then sew closer for **circle over an intersection** matches. When the circle completes itself

Photo 25A - Press away the seam allowances of long thin pattern pieces with the tip of the iron.

away. When the next pattern piece is sewn on, this seam allowance will be moved aside (Photo 25A). If the iron trick doesn't work, try taking out the last few sewn stitches, and the seam allowance can then be pressed out of the way.

Here is another way to deal with long, thin pattern pieces. When the seam is about 1/4" from the end, start pivoting the seam outward at an angle (Photo 25B). When the seam allowance is ironed, it will fall back and out of the way for the next seam.

Chain piecing speeds up sewing tremendously. You may not want to try this with the first section sewn, but it really does speed up

(for example, the two large sections with half of a flower in each), peel back the edge of the pattern piece on top and visualize where the 1/4" will fall. Then, place a pin at that intersection. This is similar to the way points are matched in traditional piecing.

During construction, pin **circle match notations** first, then worry about aligning the end points of the pattern pieces. I also find it helpful to remove the paper when matching **circles over intersections**. The **circle over the intersection** notation is a seam matching point. It is sometimes hard to see where to pin the color change at that seam. If needed, the pattern pieces can be ironed on again.

Long, thin pattern pieces sometimes produce odd seam allowances. To get a seam back and out of the way, try using the tip of the iron to push the seam allowance

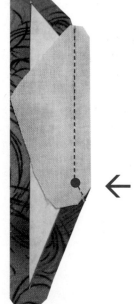

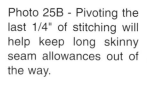

Photo 25B - Pivoting the last 1/4" of stitching will help keep long skinny seam allowances out of the way.

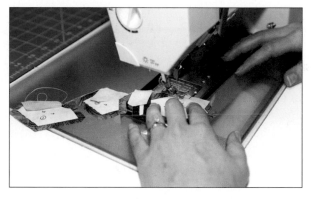

Photo 25C - Chain stitching pairs speeds up sewing.

the process. As soon as you become comfortable finding "pairs," you are ready to try it. (Photo 25C).

When the pattern pieces are displayed on the tray, randomly select one. Check it on the Master Pattern to see which pattern piece can be sewn to one side to make a pair. Pin this pair, fold back and finger press the sewing crease, and set it up on the sewing machine. Don't sew it yet. Select another pattern piece, and pin it's pair. If you select a pattern piece that cannot be sewn at this time, place it along the top of the plastic tray. By following this method, you will not waste time picking up the same pattern piece again.

Continue this process with the remaining pattern pieces until you have been through all of the **circled numbers** on the tray. There will be a small stack of pattern pieces on the sewing machine for you to stitch. Chain stitch the pairs, iron the seams to one side,

Photo 26A - Iron seam line down before pinning.

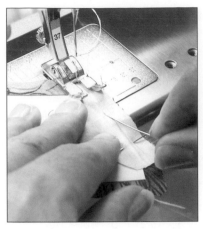

Photo 26B - Try dragging a straight pin along the seam edge to find the sewing line.

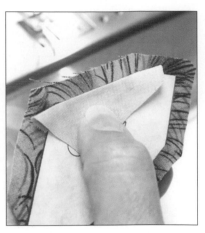

Photo 26C - Align the pattern piece by folding back the seam with your finger to obtain a guide line.

trim any "dog ears" or uneven edges, and lay them out on the plastic tray again. Go through the same assembly process, and add whatever pattern pieces you can to the original pairs. This saves you time in sewing and ironing, and eliminates the pattern pieces you have to search through the next time because there are fewer pattern pieces to work with.

After sewing, it is important to check to see that the outside edges of the freezer paper visually line up (Figure 26). If freezer paper is not straight, remove the offending piece and reposition it. If the edges of the section are aligned, it will make the next section easier to sew along the 1/4" fold. Trim threads and dog ears as you go. When joining large sections, it helps to trim these long seams using a quilters' ruler to 1/4" seam. Neatness helps tremendously.

Troubleshooting

Before ripping a sewn seam try some of these techniques:

- Some fabrics are easier to see along the folded line than others. If you are having trouble seeing the fold, try ironing the seam back along the freezer paper on the individual pattern pieces. Sew along the pressed edge. (Photo 26A).

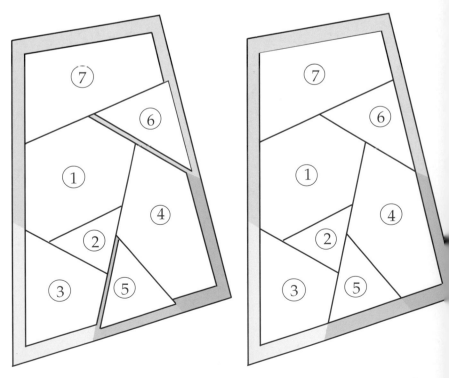

Figure 26 - Check outside pattern pieces to make sure they line up visually. Remove the offending pieces (above left) or reposition them (above right).

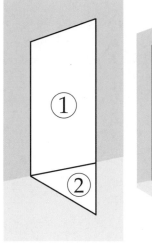
Try seaming two strips of fabric together and iron the pattern pieces on.

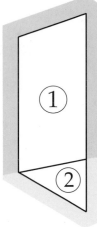

Figure 27A - Two strips of fabric can be seamed and pressed. Cut a pair as one piece and place over the sewn seam and iron. Cut out leaving seam allowance.

- Try dragging a pin along the edge of the paper (before the needle gets to it) while you are sewing. The indentation helps to see where the paper is (Photo 26B).

- If you are still having trouble seeing where to sew, try folding back the seam of the top pattern piece with your finger, and align it. Lift the seam allowance of the pattern piece on top, align, and then sew along the folded line (Photo 26C).

- Still having trouble seeing where to sew? Try having a margarita, you are way too tense! Seriously, try sewing a skinny seam and then remove the pattern pieces and reposition them with the iron.

- If small pattern pieces are causing problems, try sewing together two scraps of fabric large enough to accommodate the pattern pieces and press the seam allowance to one side. With the fabric right side up, iron the pattern pieces next to each other, with edges touching the seam. Cut them out as one piece. (Figure 27A).

- Small pattern pieces can also be avoided by sewing a scrap of fabric onto the larger pattern piece, pressing the smaller pattern piece in position and, then cutting away the excess (Figure 27B).

- You can go one step further with this idea. Go through the section and note which fab-

rics are pairs, and plan to work with them this way. Do not cut those pairs apart. Cut them as one pattern piece. Place the pattern line along the sewn seam and press. I don't do this, but it does work for some of my students. It takes time and planning to work out the combinations of colors. As you become more familiar with the technique, you begin to realize that the freezer paper pieces can be easily be removed and realigned; therefore, small pattern pieces are not so intimidating.

- If your sewn seam goes over the freezer paper slightly and paper is caught in the seam, gently tug on both sides of the seam.

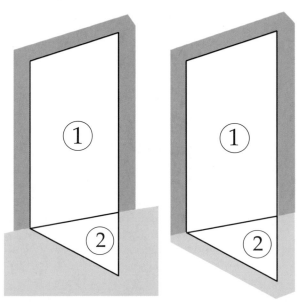

Figure 27B - A scrap can be sewn to a larger pattern piece. Then, iron the small one on and cut away.

Tip:

When repositioning pattern pieces -- first, iron the fabric flat, then press the pieces back on, one at a time. It helps to use the tip of a finger to hold the pattern piece in place.

Usually the freezer paper will release itself. Remove excess paper from the seam allowance on the back, before sewing another seam. Otherwise, it will be buried and will be impossible to get to.

If tugging doesn't work, try refolding the paper back along the edge to obtain a new fold. Resew along this fold, and then take out the original seam.

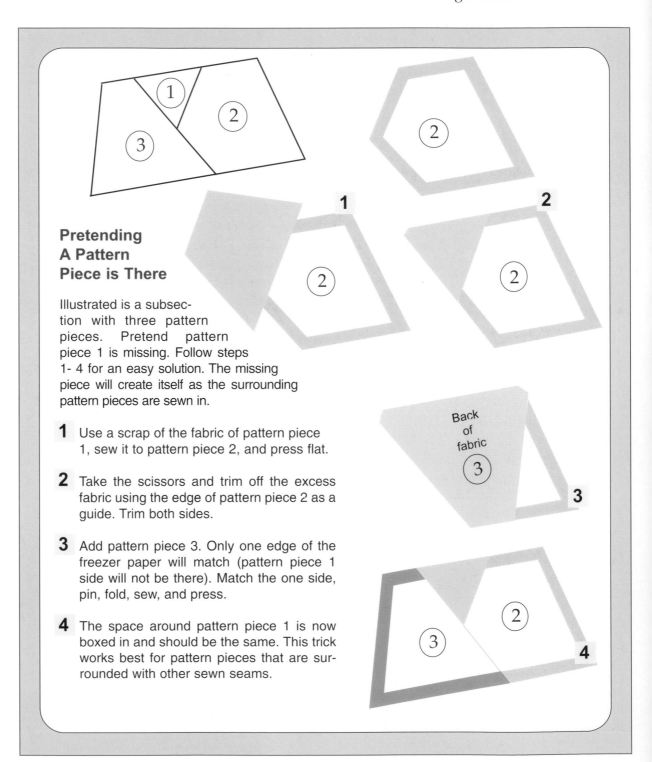

Pretending A Pattern Piece is There

Illustrated is a subsection with three pattern pieces. Pretend pattern piece 1 is missing. Follow steps 1- 4 for an easy solution. The missing piece will create itself as the surrounding pattern pieces are sewn in.

1 Use a scrap of the fabric of pattern piece 1, sew it to pattern piece 2, and press flat.

2 Take the scissors and trim off the excess fabric using the edge of pattern piece 2 as a guide. Trim both sides.

3 Add pattern piece 3. Only one edge of the freezer paper will match (pattern piece 1 side will not be there). Match the one side, pin, fold, sew, and press.

4 The space around pattern piece 1 is now boxed in and should be the same. This trick works best for pattern pieces that are surrounded with other sewn seams.

- Do not panic if a pattern piece is misplaced. Place freezer paper (shiny side down) over your Master Pattern, and trace that single piece.

- If a pattern piece is missing, you can also pretend that the pattern piece is still there. Sounds weird, I know. All seam lines are straight. If the surrounding pattern pieces are sewn, eventually the empty space takes the form of the missing pattern piece. Try it. Instructions are to the left.

- When repositioning pattern pieces, first, iron the fabric flat, then press the pattern pieces back on, one at a time. Use the tip of a finger to hold the pattern piece in place.

- If a seam needs to be tightened up, remove the paper near it, sew closer to the fold, then press the pattern pieces on again.

> **Tip:**
> *Leave the corners and some of the edge pattern pieces on after sewing a section. You will need them to reference the surrounding sections.*

Completed Sections

After a section is complete, remove as much paper as possible. Remove those pieces that are surrounded by sewn seams. You can also take off any pattern pieces that are on the outside edges that are not needed for reference (Figure 29B). The freezer paper pattern can be used again. As the pattern pieces are removed from the fabric place them in a zipper-type sandwich bag. Label it with the major section letter, or put the pattern piece with the bold section letter facing out when it is placed in the bag.

Leave on pattern pieces that must be referred to later; for example, leave the corners and edge pattern pieces. Some quilters like to leave all of the pattern pieces on until the very end. I find they get in my way. If the pattern pieces are left on until all sewing is completed, and later, you realize that the wrong fabric is mistakenly sewn in, it will be more difficult to correct. Mistakes are easier to correct as they occur rather than waiting until the last seam.

After major sections are complete, look for two sections that share a common side. Join the sections by sewing the common seam. Complete the design by joining the rest of the major sections in the same manner. Remove all freezer paper, and square up the design using a rotary cutter and ruler.

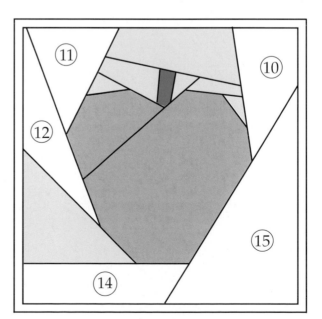

Figure 29A - Locate all pairs within a section. Pattern pieces 1 and 2, 5 and 6, 7 and 8 are all pairs and can be sewn together.

Figure 29B - Remove any pattern pieces that will not be needed for reference for the next section.

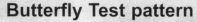

Butterfly Test pattern

Before learning the design aspects of the technique, it is best to familiarize yourself with how the technique works. Take the time to practice sewing. It will give you a better understanding of how designs must be sectioned. Following is a quick and easy test pattern for you to try.

First, trace the butterfly pattern provided (Figure 31) onto plastic coated freezer paper, shiny side down. Look for freezer paper in your local quilt shop or the grocery store. Often it is located near the canning supplies. If you haven't used freezer paper for quilting purposes before, note that the back side is shiny and has a wax coating. This wax coating sticks to the fabric when heated with an iron. Place the freezer paper (shiny side down) on top of the pattern (Figure 31). You will be able to see the pattern through the freezer paper. With a pencil and straight edge, trace all lines and notations. The pattern traced will be cut apart and The Butterfly Test Pattern (facing page) will be used as your Master Pattern.

Freezer paper patterns can be used multiple times. The pattern traced on freezer paper will be cut apart and used as templates. After sewing the block, save the pattern pieces by placing each section in your labeled zipper-type sandwich bag if you want to use them again.

Note: All *England Design* patterns have pre-printed freezer paper included. This tracing step is eliminated if you are working with an *England Design* pattern. When working with your own design, you will draw on freezer paper then make a photocopy to use as a master pattern.

A few differences between Picture Piecing and foundation piecing are:

- In Picture Piecing there is no fabric waste because you cut out exactly what you need. In foundation piecing, scraps of fabrics are used and the surplus is then cut away.

- Seams are made next to the freezer paper, rather than through it; therefore, there is no paper to remove from the seams. If foundation piecing with paper, all paper must be removed from the seams when finished.

- In Picture Piecing, pattern pieces are ironed on the right side of the fabric, rather than the wrong side. This enables you to use the fabric to the best advantage. For example, if there is a directional fabric or a striped fabric in foundation piecing, you have to guess which way to flip it. In Picture Piecing, there is no guessing. What you see is what you get.

- Any two pattern pieces that make a pair can be sewn together. This enables chain stitching within a section, making construction faster. Different parts of one section can be worked on simultaneously, whereas foundation piecing requires sewing one pattern piece at a time.

- The best reason for using the Picture Piecing technique: *cheating is allowed and is encouraged!* If the seam is not sewn close enough to the edge of the paper, reposition the pattern piece and iron it again.

Basic Pattern Notations

① **Circled numbers** identify pattern pieces and indicate the order in which they are sewn.

A **Bold letters and bold lines** indicate major sections. Sew these sections individually.

---- **Dashed lines** indicate subsections within a major section.

B **Fabric notations** are shown with letters.

→ **Arrows** denote which way to place pattern pieces when ironing on directional fabric.

To the left is a legend of basic pattern notations. Organize fabrics by making a color chart. Clip a small swatch of each fabric. Attach them to a piece of paper with a glue stick and label them with the corresponding letter notation.

W - wings   **B** - sky   **G** - body

Figure 31 - Test Pattern

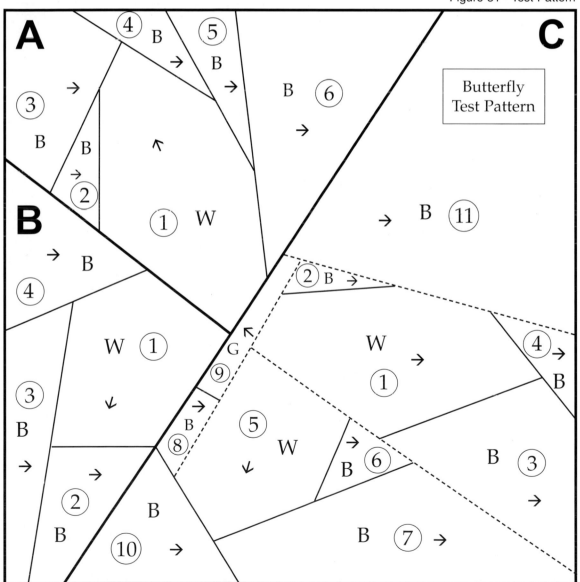

Photo 32
Lighthouse   2004   33" X 29"
Cynthia England

This wall hanging is a compilation of several different photographs of ligthhouses. The back of a red and white stripe fabric was used to make the sailboat appear in the distance. The perfect water fabric was used to indicate the waves hitting the rocks. When ironing the pattern pieces on, the "splash" printed on the fabric was intentionally placed next to the rocks to make it look more realistic. To add contrast between the llighthouse and the sky, a gray stem stitch was embroidered along the seam.

Photo 33
Positano, Italy Coastline   1998   50" x 42"
Cynthia England

This quilt was based on a composite of photographs from a special vacation. Details were given as to which buildings were visited and instructions given to emphasize them. The quilt was made over a period of four months and has approximately 6,700 pieces created from 144 different fabrics. Private Collection.
Photograph by Richard Margolis.

Chapter Four

Designing

Now that you know the basics of how to sew, let's move on to designing your own project. Make sure you are passionate about your subject. You will become intimately involved with it. Look for subject matter that has high contrast, movement, and draws the viewer in. When considering subjects, ask yourself what it is about that particular photograph that appeals to you? Is it the colors, the setting, or a particular object? Play up the aspect that drew your attention in the first place. Make it a goal to re-create that interest point for the viewer. I rarely use a photograph exactly as it appears; usually changes are made, by omission or by adding other elements.

Your quilt can start with virtually anything - a favorite greeting card, a calendar photograph, or a magazine clipping. In art school, we were taught to keep a "morgue file". You may be keeping a morgue file and are unaware of it. A morgue file contains magazine clippings and printed matter. Before throwing away old magazines, go through them. Clip out interesting photographs, colorations, objects, anything that catches your eye. Sort and file the clippings. Label the files - animals, landscapes, flowers, and so on.

Photo 34 - Detail
Split Rail
Cynthia England

A kitten peeks through the slats of the rough-hewn fence. Full view of the quilt is on Page 37.

Now you have a morgue file which becomes your own "library" that you can reference. The local library is also a good source for photographs, especially the children's section.

Digital photography offers wonderful benefits. Through your computer you can superimpose elements from one photograph onto another. Colors can be enhanced and altered; backgrounds changed. A morgue file library can be set up in computer files as well.

It is important to respect copyright laws. When working from someone else's photograph, make an effort to contact them to obtain permission to use the photo.

Choosing Your Subject

When designing a wall hanging of a vase of roses, I gather many pictures of roses and go through them to find the most interesting ones. Then, I use tracing paper and outline the individual parts that appeal to me, and "arrange" these outline drawings to form my own design. It is just like arranging flowers, using outline drawing components.

When planning a landscape piece of an interesting period house, I take photos of the house at many different angles, and at different times of the day, selecting the one that is most interesting. Objects can be eliminated if the design works better. There may be a dead

Photo - 36A
Try taking photographs at odd angles. Look "up" into the trees.
Photograph by Leroy Williamson

tree right in front of the house which blocks the doorway. Eliminate it from the line drawing. An interesting tree from another photo can be superimposed over the original. Then, the tree line drawing can be rearranged to create the most interesting composition.

Take photographs at interesting angles and vantage points (Photo 36A). Never place the main interest in a design in the center. The goal is to have the viewer's eye move around the entire quilt rather than get "stuck" in one place. Frequently, part of a subject is more interesting than the whole. Try cropping photographs on your computer or cut a frame out of paper and move it around your photograph to see what works best (Photos 36B and 36C).

Hang the picture up and study it. Pay attention to what is background, foreground,

Photos 36B and 36C
Cropping allows you to focus attention on a subject. The photo above is the cropped version of the one at right. The pelican and the turtles are now more the center of interest.
Photograph by L. Williamson

36 • Designing

Photo 37 - *Split Rail*   1995   26" x 38"   Cynthia England
Lighting on the fence became the focal point for this quilt. Private Collection.
Photograph by Mellisa Karlin Mahoney courtesy of *Quilter's Newsletter Magazine*.

and which subjects, if any, can be created with applique or paint. Objects in the foreground usually require more detail, resulting in smaller pieces. In a field of flowers, you might randomly choose some in the foreground to detail. In the background, you may want to use fabric that indicates flowers and then paint in details and embroider others. Each quilt is different, and what you can accomplish depends on the detail of the subject matter and how large a quilt you decide to make. The larger the quilt, the more detail you can put into it.

When working from actual photographs, make photocopies to work from. It is helpful to make a color copy and a black and white copy. The black and white copy will help with fabric selection and will help to show high contrast areas at a glance. Use the color copy for color reference and as a way to preserve the original. Color copies can be modified to create different effects. If your photograph has an overcast sky, it can be brightened. Tell the operator of the machine which color to enhance, with a push of a button, the sky can be clear.

When selecting your fabric, consider the following:

- Select as many different textures as possible.
- Vary the scales and prints of the fabrics.
- Make use of the back of fabrics for subtle variations.
- Light, medium, and dark shades are required to create light and shadow effects. A single fabric that varies in color can offer several fabric choices.
- For realism, aim for a natural gradation from one color to the next. Tone-on-tone fabrics generally work best for shading.
- Try to keep background fabrics toned down. Busy fabrics detract from the main subject matter. Avoid directional fabrics for backgrounds.
- Stay away from geometric prints. Strong patterns tend to demand attention.

Textures

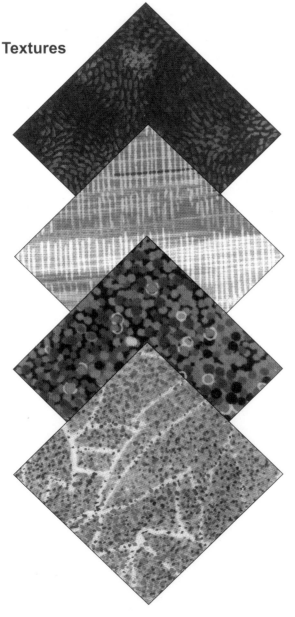

Selecting Fabrics

This is my favorite part - picking the fabrics! We are so fortunate to have many beautiful fabrics at our disposal. Don't forget to consider fabrics other than cottons for your art quilt. Satins, organzas, mock suedes, and other textured fabric will add interest to your finished piece. Make sure the fabric can be ironed with a cotton setting without melting. Try to use primarily cottons, but add others for special accents. Examples of good fabrics of varying scale and texture are shown in the swatches on the left.

Be careful with strong geometric prints like the examples below. They attract too much attention.

Strong geometric fabrics are hard to blend and will demand attention.

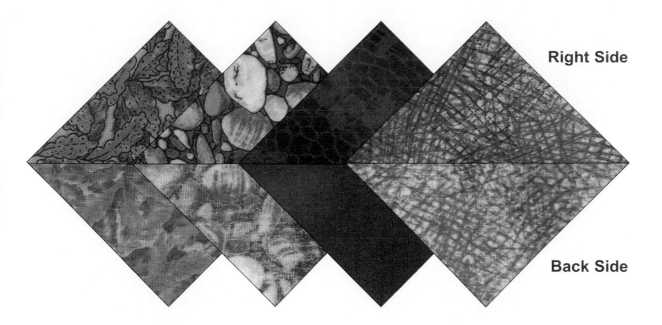

Using the Back of the Fabric

Look closely at your fabric. You can increase your stash by making use of the subtle color gradations on the back. If you are using the front and back of a fabric, cut two swatches and place them according to their shades on the color chart. The fabric color and the process used to print it determine the imprint of the back. Batik fabrics look similar on both sides. Woven fabrics, such as plaids, look the same on the back as well. Sometimes backs are very fuzzy. Try to think of the color as texture rather than a print. *Southwest Splendor* (Photos 39A and 39B) uses the front and the back of the same beige fabric to depict the desert. A light fabric containing texture was needed for the ground cover. Darker shades are indicated by using the front of the fabric.

Distance can be indicated using the back of a fabric (especially leafy fabrics). They appear fuzzy and out of focus and will give that "far away" look.

Backs of printed plaids work well to indicate sashing for windows. If the back of the fabric is out of focus, you can paint details in, or use a fine-line permanent marker to redefine them.

Photo 39A and 39B -
Southwest Splendor   2001   21" x 18"
Cynthia England
The back and front of the same beige fabric were used for desert in *Southwest Splendor*. This subtle fabric was directional.

Sort fabrics by color gradation. The fabric swatches pictured below left, need to be sorted. The fabrics on the right are the same fabrics, sorted from light to dark. After your fabrics have been organized, cut a swatch of each and use a glue stick to paste them to a piece of paper. Label them in order of shade. In the example below, G1 would be the lightest and G5 the darkest.

Tip:
When sorting fabrics for a pictorial quilt, lay them out from light to dark by color value. Avoid fabrics that "jump out at you" or purchase others to provide a gradation from one to the next. I sort by color family; for example, yellow greens versus blue greens.

Unsorted

Sorted

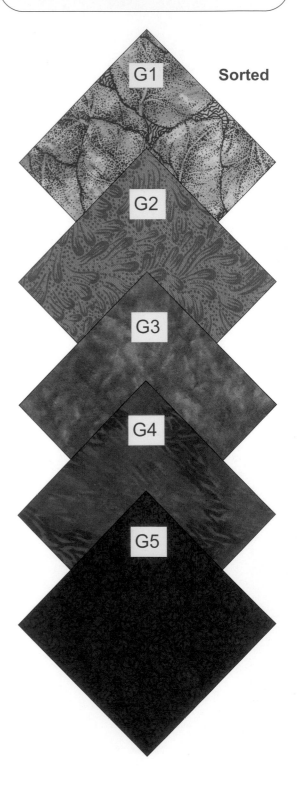

 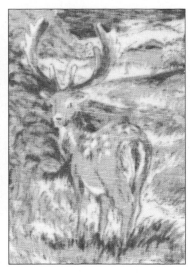

Photos 41A and 41B - Details
Piece and Quiet
Cynthia England
The original fabric used for the deer in *Piece and Quiet* is at the far left. When the fabric was reversed it changed the direction the deer was facing.

In *Piece and Quiet* (Page 9) there are two printed animal fabrics pieced into the quilt top. I had a deer fabric that I liked, but it had gold metallic flecks on it and the deer was facing the wrong direction. I wanted the deer facing into the quilt, not looking out. I reversed the fabric and sewed it in. Definition was added with paint washes and a permanent marker. This worked well because I could then "camouflage" the deer using paint colors that matched the fabrics which surrounded it (Photos 41A - 41C).

Representational

Photo 41C - Detail, *Piece and Quiet*
Cynthia England
The deer fabric was pieced in and then redefined with washes of paint and permanent marker.

Figures 42A and 42B - The fabric used to indicate the path on the left is too literal. Perspective is lost. The path on the right gives a more realistic look. Larger rocks can be made using thread or marker in the foreground.

Representational Fabrics

Be careful when selecting representational fabrics. By representational fabric I am referring to fabrics that look like specific things, for example, grass, rocks, flowers, bricks, and so on (Page 41). There is a fine line between "cutesy" and "classy." I buy many of these types of fabrics. A good collection of various sized flowers, grasses, and nature-related fabrics is necessary to indicate realism in a landscape. Keep in mind the scale and perspective of the design. For example, when working on a garden scene with a rock path that fades into the distance, do not use a distinctive rock in the front **and** the back. It loses perspective (Figure 42A). In real life, the stones would appear smaller the farther away they are

from the viewer. It is better to use a rock fabric that indicates stone rather than a more literal interpretation (Figure 42B). Details can be added in the foreground by painting some of the rocks that appear closer or outlining and redefining with markers or paints to add interest. The example above made use of the back of a stone fabric. If realism is the goal, scale makes a big difference in how successful your quilt becomes. Match fabrics to the scale of the larger items in your picture. For example, in Photo 42B, the size of the leaves in the tree foliage are too large for the tree's scale. In the photo to the left , the scale of the leaf fabric in the tree is more in tune with the rest of the design. Details count, and viewers notice.

Photo 42A and 42B
Country Road   1996   17" x 19"
Cynthia England
Match the scale of motifs to the scale of the size of the object. In the example above, the leaves are too large in comparison to the tree. The scale of the leaf fabric on the left is more realistic.

Photo 43A and 43B
Ambush
48" x 35"   2002
Rhonda Gabriel

Rhonda lives on the waterfront in scenic Canyon Lake, Texas. For her first original pattern she decided to make a quilt with black bass for her husband, who is an avid fisherman. He provided color suggestions and critiqued her design for realism. Actual fishing line and a real hook were used to accent her quilt.

Chapter Five

Sectioning

Sectioning refers to the process of changing a line drawing into straight lines. When sewing, it is easier to stitch a straight line. Curved lines require easing and careful pinning to maintain the curve. Straight lines make construction faster and set-in seams can be eliminated.

A full-size line drawing of the subject is the starting point for sectioning. It helps to familiarize yourself with how a design must be constructed before actually sectioning the line drawing. Throughout this chapter you will find many examples. Use them as a guide to practice sectioning.

Bear in mind that I am mathematically challenged. I am aware that some of the designing process contains math elements, but I prefer not to think of them in those terms. For those of you who are friends of math, I apologize. To the others, well, you can relate.

Photo 44 - Detail
Open Season
Cynthia England

The actual height of this pieced rabbit is five inches. Permanent marker was used for detail work. Full view of quilt is on Page 61. Photograph by C. England.

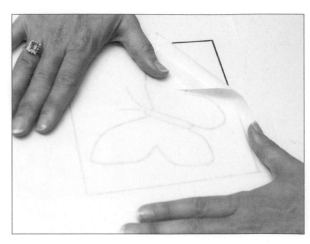

Making a Line Drawing

To section a line drawing, you will work with layers. The line drawing will be placed facing up on the tabletop, and freezer paper with the shiny side down on top of that (Photo 46A). All pattern notations are made on the freezer paper. The line drawing underneath becomes a guide for the drawing foundation. For illustration purposes of this book, line drawings will be in shades of color. Keep in mind that freezer paper is always on top of the line drawing during sectioning.

When determining fabric notations, use the photograph as a reference. Keep the fabric selection chart close at hand. Colored pencils or markers can differentiate objects in the line

Photo 46A - Place freezer paper (shiny side down) on top of the line drawing. All notations are made on the freezer paper.

drawing. They are also helpful for indicating shading. Any coloring should be done on the line drawing rather than the freezer paper. Colored pencils and markers were used on the line drawing (Photo 46B) to help with the shading of the *Blood, Sweat and Flowers* border design (facing page). I do not usually shade line drawings. I use the photograph and try to re-create colors in fabric. However, coloring the line drawing can be helpful when a photo is not readily available.

Photo 46B and 46C
Markers and colored pencils were used on the line drawing of *Blood, Sweat and Flowers*' border to help with fabric selection. Photographs by C. England.

Photo 47

Blood, Sweat and Flowers   1997   80" x 102"   Cynthia England

Photographs were referenced to create the most realistic birds and flowers possible. Before quilting became my primary focus, gardening occupied a lot of my time. The "Blood" reference in the name of the quilt is due to the labor-intensive pieced border. It took longer to sew than all of the flowers and birds. Patterns are available for the center blocks. Photograph by Mellisa Karlin Mahoney, courtesy of *Quilter's Newsletter Magazine*.

Figure 48A shows three drawings at 50%, 100%, and 150%. Keep in mind that 100% is actual size.

After deciding on the subject, a full-size line drawing is required. To do this, place tracing paper over the photocopy and draw an outline of the main elements. For example, if you are creating a landscape similar to *Garden Path* (Photo 48), draw the tree, the path, the bench, and so on (Figure 48B).

If you have combined several line drawings to create your design, make one final line drawing incorporating those changes. Make thumbnail design sketches to choose from. It is much easier to make composition changes at the thumbnail stage than full size.

Using a Proportional Scale

What size do you want your quilt to be? You may not care, or you may have a certain wall in your home where you would like the quilt to be displayed. One artist's tool that is helpful to determine the size of a quilt is a proportional scale. They are inexpensive and can be found at art supply stores. The proportional scale is made up of two plastic circles joined in the center with a metal connector. On the outside of both circles are number increments. There is a window in the smaller circle that shows you the percentage required to achieve the size desired (Photo 49). Keep in mind that 100% represents full size and 50% is half size (Figure 48A).

Photo 48
Garden Path   Cynthia England   2001   21" x 18"

Figure 48B
The line drawing consists of an simplified outline of the main elements.

To use a proportional scale, determine the width desired for your finished quilt; for example, 60" wide. Measure the finished width of the original line drawing (8 1/2"). Line up 8 1/2" on the inner circle (which is the original size) to the 60" on the outer circle (the desired finished size). Look in the window to find out what percentage the line drawing must be enlarged. It is approximately 710%. Some copy machines enlarge only up to 141%. Continue enlarging the design until the size at the highest percentage yields the size the outline drawing must be.

This tool is helpful for traditional quilting patterns also. If you have a quilting design that measures 8" x 8" but you have an alternate block space that measures 12" x 12", you can line up the 8" to the 12" on the proportional scale and determine that you need to enlarge the quilting pattern 150% to obtain the right size. To reduce the design, simply reverse the process. If you have a 12" quilting pattern and want to make it fit an 8" pattern, line up the 12" on the outside circle and 8" on the inside circle. The design

must be reduced by 67%.

To use the Picture Piecing technique, the line drawing must be full size. I have one wall in my studio that has a 2 1/2 - inch grid drawn on it and is numbered along the top, bottom, and down the middle. I use this to enlarge line drawings. It also doubles as a tool to square up finished quilts.

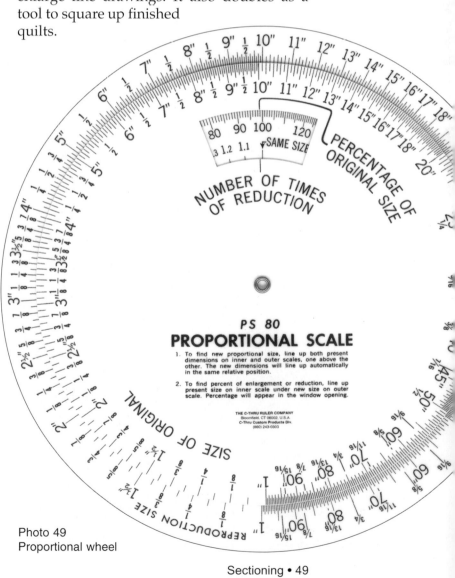

Photo 49
Proportional wheel

Tip:

You can use other measurements when working with the proportional wheel. If you have trouble with fractions, try the pica or the centimeter side of the ruler instead. The ratio will still be the same.

Photo 50A
Mallard Duck   1999   17" x 17"   Cynthia England
If elements of the design overlap the border such as the cattails in this pattern, they must be included in the initial line drawing.

Enlarging the Pattern

The line drawing does not have to be perfect. It can be loosely sketched and when taped together, the lines do not have to match perfectly. This line drawing goes under the freezer paper when the actual pattern is sectioned and provides a basis for your line work. Important lines are made on the freezer paper rather than on the actual line drawing.

Photo 50B
Squirrel   1999   17" x 17"   Cynthia England

After determining the size of the quilt, draw an outline of the finished dimensions. Seam allowances are added when cutting out fabric. Therefore, this outline is the actual size, before adding borders. If you plan on adding elements that overlap the border and you want to piece them in, those borders must be included in the original line drawing. On the left side of *Mallard Duck* (Photo 50A), one reed overlaps the left border and a cattail overlaps the top border. The line drawing includes the left and top borders. The other two borders are sewn on traditionally.

Layering the Freezer Paper

Regardless of the size of the project, the line drawing must be enlarged to full size. After the line drawing is enlarged cover it with a layer of freezer paper. All pattern markings are made on the freezer paper. It can be taped together to accommodate large designs. Lay the freezer paper over the line drawing to determine the length needed. Tear the freezer paper from the roll the length of the wall hanging or section you are work-

Ways to enlarge the design:

- Use the grid system by making a small grid on acetate. Number the grid across the top, side and down the middle. Place it over your original line drawing, then enlarge it by marking corresponding lines on a larger grid that has been numbered in the same manner.
- Project a slide on a large piece of paper on the wall.
- Use an opaque projector to transfer the small line drawing to a larger one.
- Photocopy it to the size desired. You can do it yourself and tape the enlarged design together. If you have a business nearby that handles large copies, that is a good option. Find one that specializes in architectural blueprint copies. Ask the price before the enlargement is made. Prices vary considerably. It requires quite a bit of time to copy and tape together a line drawing of this size, even if you have your own copier.

ing on (Figure 51A). The outside edges of freezer paper are machine cut so they will be straight. Place two sheets side by side with the shiny sides up. Butting them together, use small pieces of drafting tape to lightly tack the two sheets along the seam (Figure 51B). Flip the two sheets over to the dull paper side, placing transparent tape lengthwise along the seam. Make sure the tape runs from end to end and has no spaces between it (Figure 51C). The pattern will be cut into pieces. If there are spaces between the tape, it will fall apart. Flip the freezer paper back over, and remove the small pieces of drafting tape from the shiny side. The finished large sheet of freezer paper will now have tape only on the dull paper side. When ironing, the tape may shrivel slightly, but it should not leave residue on the iron. Take care not to hold the iron down on the tape too long. You may find it helpful to retrace those pattern pieces with the tape on them, eliminating the careful handling of those pattern pieces.

Large projects can be overwhelming; it helps to work on them in sections. Place freezer paper along one end of the line drawing and separate a large portion to work with. Divide it up, mark **color notations** and **placement numbers**, then photocopy it. The drawing process can become tedious. Breaking the line drawing into workable sections enables intervals for sewing. After all, it is the sewing we enjoy most!

As the project gets further along, certain fabrics will be more appealing than others. When marking **fabric color notations** on new sections, take this opportunity to either add more of your favorite fabrics or gradually eliminate some that you do not like. Sprinkle fabrics in or out when introducing or eliminating new shades. Gradually doing this blends the colors. The larger the project, the more time it will take to make. New fabrics are introduced frequently, and this is a good way to work them in.

Figure 51A - Lay the freezer paper over the line drawing.

Figure 51B - Butt them together, machine-cut edges next to each other.

Figure 51C - join the two pieces together to make one large sheet.

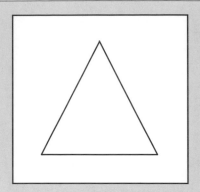

Figure 52A - Begin with a line drawing.

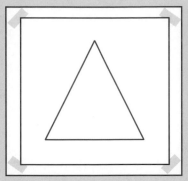

Figure 52B - Place freezer paper over the line drawing and tape.

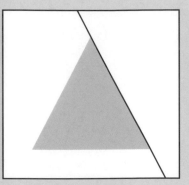

Figure 52C - On the freezer paper, draw the first line from the edge.

Sectioning Straight Lines

Designs can be sectioned many different ways. There is not a magical number of sections or a formula to determine the number of pattern pieces that go in each section. The most common mistake is dividing the design too much, which requires sewing extra seams.

The goal of this process is to remove all curves so the design can be sewn by machine with straight lines only, eliminating set-in seams. The important lines are the ones in pencil that will be made on the dull paper side of the freezer paper. Keep an eraser handy.

To practice, section out this simple triangle (Figure 52A). Place freezer paper over the line drawing, shiny side down (Figure 52B). You will be able to see through the freezer paper to the line drawing underneath. It will not be as transparent as tracing paper, but the

line drawing will be visible. If the line drawing is not clear, trace over it with a medium-sized black marker.

Use drafting tape and attach the freezer paper to the line drawing at the corners to keep them from sliding apart. Tape only to the freezer paper. Do not tape the line drawing to the table and then tape the freezer paper to the line drawing. There are times when it is helpful to move the design around to obtain different angles.

Note the outline of the box the triangle is placed in. This represents the finished size of the block or quilt. Do not start sectioning any design without indicating the parameters of your finished project. Do not draw the triangle on the freezer paper first. Move the straight edge around the design along the outline of the triangle. Draw the first line

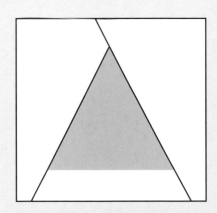

Figure 52D - Choose the upper point of the triangle and draw a line down to the edge of the box.

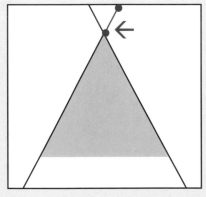

Figure 52E - ⊘ Do not start the second line from the upper edge of the box. The line between the two red dots indicates an unnecessary seam.

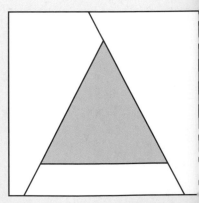

Figure 52F - A final line across the bottom completes the triangle.

from one edge of the box to the other edge of the box (Figure 52C). This line will be the last sewn seam. The first line is chosen at random. Later, as designs get more complex, there will be other considerations taken into account when drawing this first line.

Two fabric colors will be represented in this line drawing: one for the triangle and another for the background. The second line drawn can start at the top of the triangle or from the lower right corner of the triangle. Let's start from the top of the triangle (Figure 52D). There is no need to start from the upper edge of the box because that would cut through the background and make an unnecessary seam (Figure 52E). Start from the line drawn previously and place another line along the edge of the triangle. Extend it to the lower edge of the box. The last line placed extends from the right corner of the triangle to the left corner of the triangle (Figure 52F). Check to see if the drawing is completely sectioned by picking up the freezer paper's edge. If the outline of the design has been replicated on the freezer paper with straight lines, it is finished. See Figure 53A for different ways to section this simple triangle. All of these examples are correct but demonstrate variations in the process.

After sectioning lines are drawn, mark the fabric colors: T for triangle and B for background (Figure 53B). Each pattern piece is

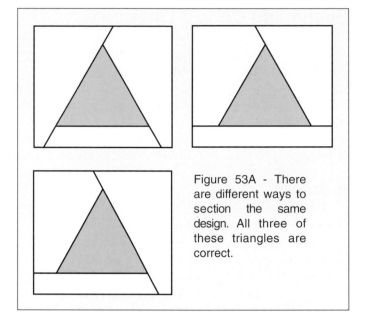

Figure 53A - There are different ways to section the same design. All three of these triangles are correct.

labeled with a **circled number** to indicate sewing sequence (Figure 53C). To decide where to begin numbering, study the line drawing. Find two pattern pieces that make a pair, or share a common seam. Label one pattern piece 1 and the other, 2. When this pair is sewn together, they will be long enough for the pattern piece to the left. The pattern piece to the left will be labeled 3. After it is sewn, the three pattern pieces combined (a subsection) are now long enough for pattern piece 4. This design consists of only four pattern pieces. Therefore, it is not necessary to worry with major sections and **dotted lines.** Add **directional arrows** if any of the fabrics have stripes or waves in them. After all notations are made (**circle placement numbers, fabric colors,** and **directional arrows**), photocopy the freezer paper pattern. Place it in the top of a copy machine like any other paper you would copy and duplicate it. Do not use the automatic feed feature on the copy machine. DON'T FORGET TO COPY IT. This is a very simple pattern. However, if a more complex pattern was cut apart before making a photocopy, you really would have a puzzle on your hands.

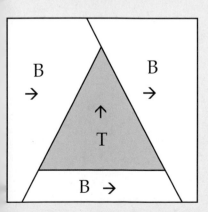

Figure 53B - **Color notations** and any **directional arrows** (if needed) are placed on each pattern piece.

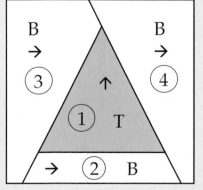

Figure 53C - **Circled placement numbers** are then added. The pattern is now ready to be photocopied.

Sectioning Curved Lines

Two ways are used to deal with curved lines. Both achieve curves, but they break the background up differently. A circle will be used as the design to demonstrate both methods. One circle will be divided by "Boxing in," and the other circle will be divided using a "Radiation" division. Remember I am math challenged, so this is my own terminology.

Boxing In

Two fabric colors will be used for this circle. One is used for the background and one for the circle. Lay freezer paper over the design and draw the outside box dimensions (Figure 54B).

Do not draw the circle on the freezer paper. Only straight lines will be placed on the freezer paper. The circle is on the line drawing under the freezer paper, and the goal is to replicate it using straight lines on the freezer paper. One of the most common mistakes seen in classes is that the circle is drawn on the freezer paper and then lines are extended as in Figure 54C.

The circle's first line is placed diagonally on the top right edge of the circle, and the second line is placed parallel to that line along the bottom left edge (Figure 55A). Third and fourth lines are placed along the sides of the circle to "box" it in (Figure 55B). Diagonal lines are placed across the edges to complete the shape (Figure 55C).

Lift the freezer paper, and you can see that the circle has been duplicated on the freezer paper, with straight lines.

When sectioning, think "folk art." Avoid making the lines too close together. There are no curved seams in this technique. Anything that appears to be a curve is actually a series of straight lines that make it look that way. The viewer's eye will make it look like the object is curving.

To number this "boxed in" circle, start by finding a pair (two pieces that share a common seam). In this circle, all pairs must begin with the straight edged circle shape in the center (Figure 55D). There are four choices of pattern pieces which can be added first. Any of the smaller triangles next to the center pattern piece can be sewn. Start by numbering the large center pattern piece 1; then, number one of the small triangles 2, and continue clockwise around the circle edges

Photo 54 - Detail
Pansy 2000
Pieced by Rosie Skowronek

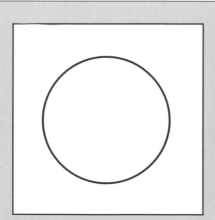

Figure 54A - Circle line drawing.

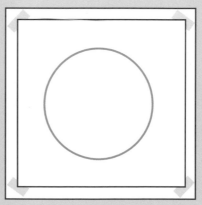

Figure 54B - Place freezer paper, shiny side down, over the line drawing.

Figure 54C- ⊘ Do not extend lines out from the circle. The circle is not on the freezer paper yet; it has to be created with straight lines.

until the four small triangles are numbered. They will be sewn one at a time to the center pattern piece. Add the upper left corner piece next. Then, add the one in the bottom right corner, and add the triangles at the other corners to complete the numbering sequence. Add **fabric notations** and **directional arrows**, if needed, then make a photocopy.

If a perfect circle is the goal, lines and pattern pieces can be placed closer together (Figure 56A). However, if lines are too close together, pattern pieces get smaller. Decide where in the design it is important to have a curve before making close divisions. One example of an important curve may be the stomach of a bird. If the stomach is left angular it may ruin the look of a delicate bird. In that case, it is better to sew a few more seams, making the bird look more realistic. Figure 56B shows three other alternatives of sectioning a circle.

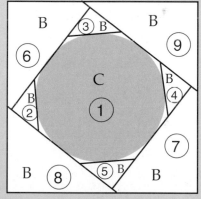

Figure 55D - Add **circled placement numbers**, **color notations**.

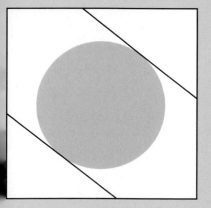

Figure 55A - Place two lines on either side of the circle along the edges.

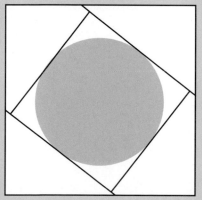

Figure 55B - Box the circle in by placing two additional lines on either side.

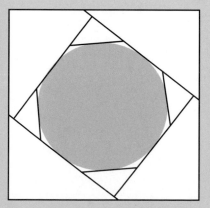

Figure 55C - Complete sectioning the circle by adding four more lines.

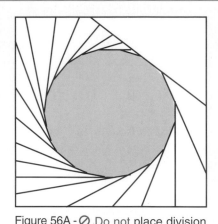

Figure 56A - ⊘ Do not place division lines too close together.

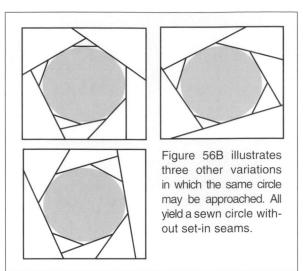

Figure 56B illustrates three other variations in which the same circle may be approached. All yield a sewn circle without set-in seams.

Radiating Division

In this example (Figure 56C), begin by making the first line from one end of the box to the other end. The second line catches the edge of the circle, to the end of the box (Figure 56D). Start pulling lines out along the edge of the circle, and extend them to the box edge (Figure 56E). Make sure that the new line begins from the one that was drawn previously. Continue in this manner until all the division lines complete the circle. The last line will touch the first line (Figure 57C). Complete the design by adding **circle placement numbers** and **fabric notations** (Figures 57D and 57E). Can you see how the background pattern pieces could change colors as in the color wheel as they go around? Radiating division works well to indicate a

shape turning. The eye follows the seam lines and rotates the circle. This is important to keep in mind: the eye follows the seams.

Because all pattern pieces are built on this center pattern base, start by numbering the center straight edged circle shape with 1. In a curve, pattern pieces usually must be sewn on one at a time. Look at the design, and find the pattern piece that is the pair to 1. It is the triangle shape above it. Label it with 2. The shape above and to the left (3) can be added after pattern piece 1 and 2 are joined. Number the other pattern pieces sequentially around the circle. The last number will be the triangle shape above the first line that was drawn. Add **fabric notations** and make a photocopy.

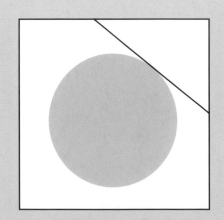

Figure 56C - First line placed on the circle line drawing.

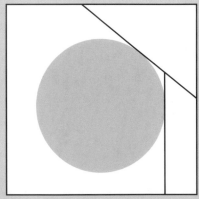

Figure 56D - Add the second line; start it from the line that was drawn previously.

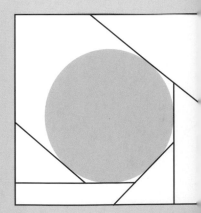

Figure 56E - Continue extendir lines out.

Figure 57A and 57B
Lines to indicate an outside curve must be made **outside** the shape (right). Lines to indicate an inside curve cut **inside** the shape (far right). They are indicated by red lines.

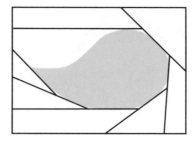

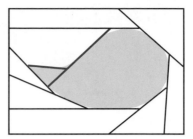

Photo 57 - Detail
Goldfinch 1996
Cynthia England

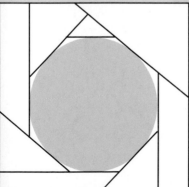

Figure 57C - Complete the circle.

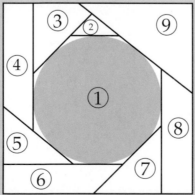

Figure 57D - Add **circled placement numbers.**

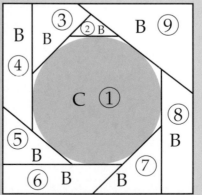

Figure 57E - Add **fabric notations** and **directional arrows** if needed.

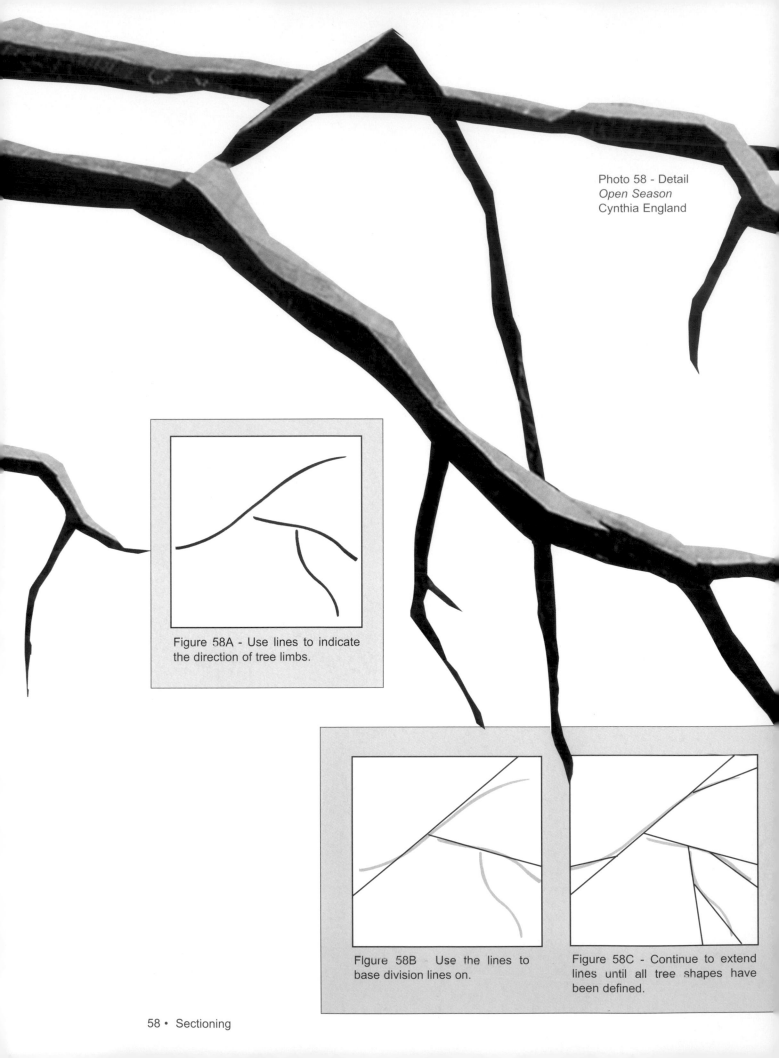

Photo 58 - Detail
Open Season
Cynthia England

Figure 58A - Use lines to indicate the direction of tree limbs.

Figure 58B Use the lines to base division lines on.

Figure 58C - Continue to extend lines until all tree shapes have been defined.

Indicating Movement

Movement can be suggested by the manner in which the line drawing is sectioned. Study the design and pay attention to how your eye follows through it. The photo will give you clues on how to start sectioning. For example, divide water the way it flows, divide a tree the way the bark grows and the way the limbs reach out.

Some subjects do not require a specific line drawing to indicate movement. When working with detailed shapes such as the many tree limbs in *Open Season* (Page 61), it can be beneficial to indicate movement rather than try to draw every limb and twig. Start by sectioning a few of the main tree limbs, then direct your attention to the smaller limbs and twigs.

In Figure 58A, three curved lines are drawn on the line drawing to represent the direction the tree limbs grow. Move the straight edge around and draw a couple of lines along the limbs directly on top of the curved lines (Figure 58B). Extend lines out for the individual branches (Figure 58C).

To make these lines look like limbs,

> **Tip:**
>
> *For intricate designs, such as tree limbs, indicate movement rather than drawing every detail.*

drop below or above them and draw lines parallel to thicken them (Figure 59A). Keep in mind that a tree limb is larger at the base of the tree and gets smaller as it grows upward. Do not keep the lines perfectly parallel. Angle limbs to get interesting shapes. When fabric colors are added and the areas shaded, you can see how the original curved lines become tree limbs (Figure 59B).

In *Open Season*, the method of using lines to indicate the direction of tree limbs was used once to thicken the tree limbs and again (above the original lines) to add snow along the tops of the branches. Trees are fun to design and provide a good learning project. It is not easy to spot a mistake among a forest because nature is very forgiving. Faces are not. Get a nose out of place or an eye too small, and it is definitely noticeable.

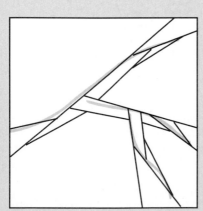

Figure 59A - "Thicken up" tree limbs by placing additional lines parallel above and below.

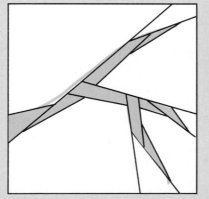

Figure 59B - When these areas are shaded you can see how limbs will form.

Photo 60
Original photograph used as reference for *Open Season* (facing page)
This photograph, taken by Leroy Williamson for *Texas Highways* magazine, became the inspiration for *Open Season*. Leroy explains the circumstances of the shot, "It was taken during an ice storm in the Texas Hill Country, on a private ranch near Canyon Lake. The snowfall was the best Texas had seen in many years and too good to let pass unphotographed. I had a lovely day on the creek in the snow and found that Texas can look a little like Colorado when conditions are right." Photograph by Leroy Williamson, courtesy of *Texas Highways* magazine.

Photo 61
Open Season   Cynthia England   2000   87" x 90"
This quilt was made over a period of six years, and it has more than 280 fabrics in it. The quilt has over 21,000 pieces. (I know because I paid my son to count them!) This is the most intricate and time-consuming quilt I have made. Photograph by Mellisa Karlin Mahoney, courtesy of *Quilter's Newsletter Magazine*.

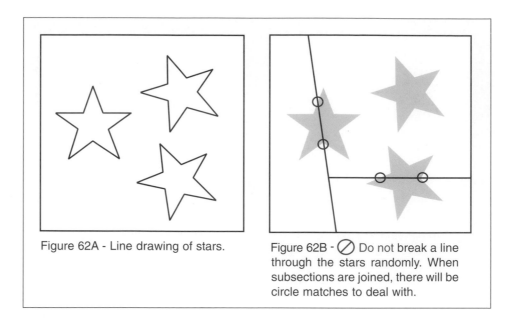

Figure 62A - Line drawing of stars.

Figure 62B - ⊘ Do not break a line through the stars randomly. When subsections are joined, there will be circle matches to deal with.

Multiple Shapes

When approaching a line drawing with multiple shapes, try to keep seam matches to a minimum. **Circle over an intersection** notations are the most difficult to sew (see Page 16). Therefore, the goal is to make as few of those notations as possible. Although these notations cannot totally be omitted, it is sometimes possible to eliminate most.

Isolating Objects

Look at the line drawing of the three stars above which seem to float on the background in Figure 62A. Try to separate the stars from one another. Do not make the first division lines directly through the stars (Figure 62B). If the lines are made this way, the stars must match at the **circle over the intersection** notations when the major sections are joined.

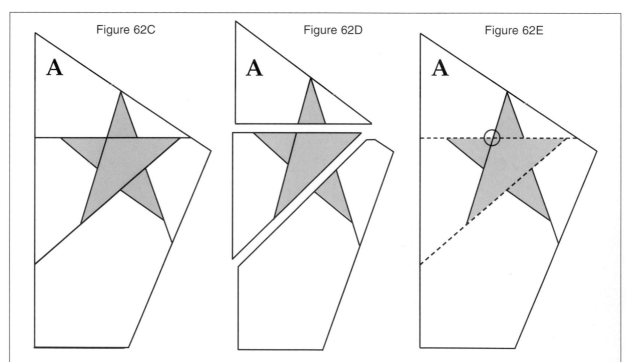

Figures 62C - 62E - To complete the star continue to extend lines out to make the outline of the star (Figure 62D). Section A consists of three subsections illustrated in Figure 62E. Dashed lines indicate subsections. **A circle over an intersection** shows an important matching point.

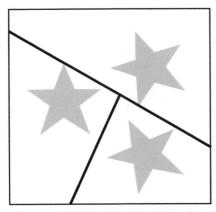

Figure 63A - Dividing the line drawing this way would be much easier. Give each group a section letter: for example, A, B, and C.

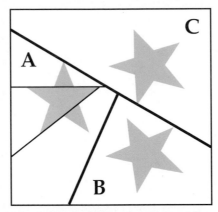

Figure 63B - Subdivide section A. Make the first line through the arms of the star. Then, extend another line going through two more arms.

If, however, the section lines are drawn away from the stars as in Figure 63A, these **circle over an intersection** notations can be eliminated. Sewing is much easier dividing it this way. The best way to deal with several shapes is to separate them from one another and deal with them one at a time.

After the first two lines are drawn, there are three separate sections. Label them A, B and C. Sections are sewn together as pairs. The two smaller sections are sewn together first (therefore, A and B were chosen), and the large one, C on the upper right side, is added after A and B are joined.

Working with section A, make one line across the star. You will have to cut through the star (Figure 63B). Going across two arms of the star will make sewing easier than cutting across randomly. If the line is haphaz-

ardly drawn, there are likely to be more **circle over an intersection** notations. Draw another line starting from the right edge of the star down across to catch the bottom left arm of the star.

Complete the star shape by extending lines out (Figure 62C). In section A there are really three subsections (Figure 62D). Three pattern pieces make up the subsection in the upper point of the star. The three pieces below them make another group, and the three pieces that make up the lower right point of the star form the third group. Use a **dashed line** along the seam to indicate these subsections (Figure 62E).

When the top subsection is joined, make sure the seams align. Use a **circle over an intersection** to indicate this match.

Photo 63 - Detail
Land That I Love
Cynthia England

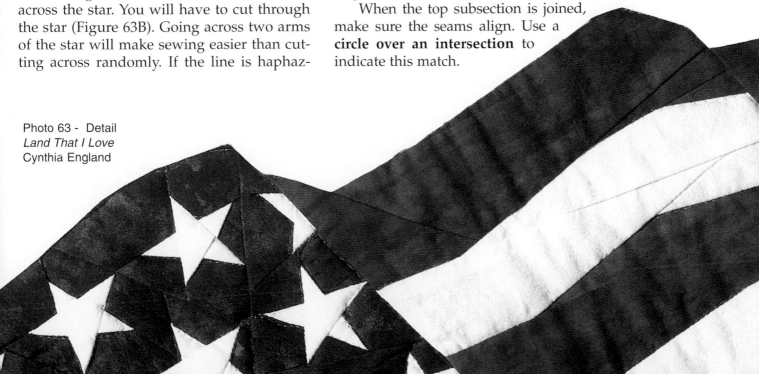

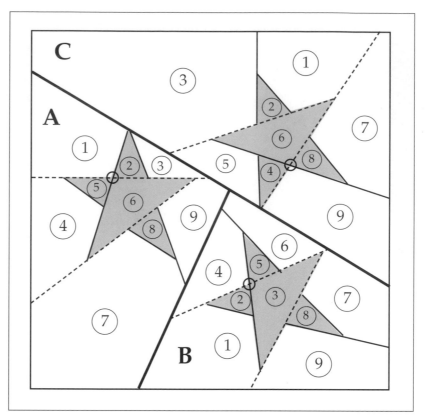

Figure 64A - Number the sections. Each section begins with a new sequence.

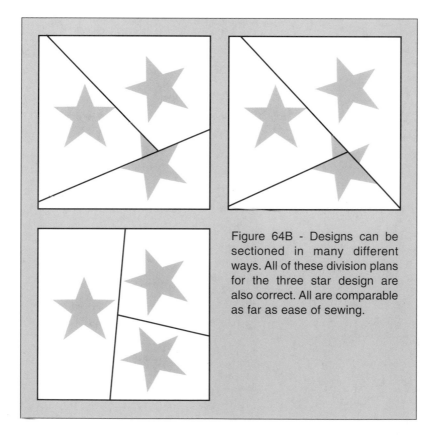

Figure 64B - Designs can be sectioned in many different ways. All of these division plans for the three star design are also correct. All are comparable as far as ease of sewing.

Divide sections B and C in the same manner (Figure 64A). Note that in each completed star there is one **circle over an intersection** match to ensure that the finished stars will be straight. Each section is **circle numbered** for placement, beginning with a new sequence for each section. Mark **fabric color notations** and **directional arrows**, if necessary. Photocopy and sew.

Figure 64B demonstrates three other ways the stars could be divided.

Figure 65A - The tree is in the foreground of this landscape line drawing.

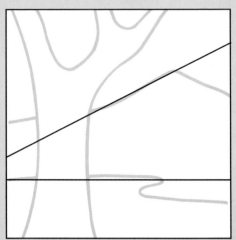

Figure 65B - ⊘ Do not use the mountain and water lines as a basis to start sectioning the design.

Figure 65C - Use the foreground shape of the tree to begin the division lines.

Overlapping Shapes

When sectioning designs with overlapping shapes, pay careful attention to which elements are in the foreground and which are in the background.

In the landscape in Figure 65A, the tree is in the foreground, and the mountain range is in the background. To emphasize this, section the design with the intent to keep the tree shape in front. Do not use the mountain shape in the background to begin the major division lines (Figure 65B). These seams will draw the eye across the tree trunk and will be distracting.

Use the foreground object (in this case, the tree) as a starting point for major division lines (Figure 65C). This pulls the viewer's eye along the base of the tree and up into the design. Continue extending lines from these major divisions to complete the drawing.

Because the tree overlaps the mountain range and the water, it is important to align these background elements. They should line up visually behind the tree as it crosses over them. Mark a **solid dot** notation on either side of the tree as a reminder to check these visual matching points during construction (Figure 65D).

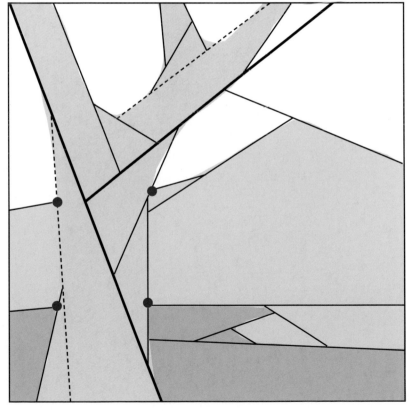

Figure 65D - Solid dots help maintain continuity under overlapping shapes.

Figure 66A - Seagull line drawing.

Figure 66B - ⊘ Do not use background shapes to initiate major divisions.

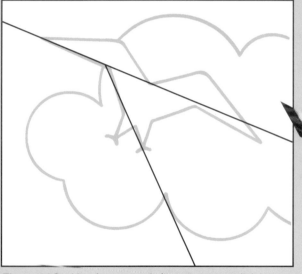

Figure 66C - Use foreground shapes to start divisions.

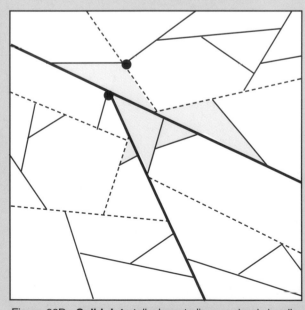

Figure 66D - **Solid dots** tell where to line up cloud visually.

Figures 66A through 66D illustrate the overlapping premise of using the object in the foreground, a seagull, as the basis for sectioning.

Photo 67A   *I Left My Heart*   2002   38" x 28"   Patty Dillon

Patty's inspiration for this quilt was her childhood home in California. She comments, "Growing up, I never really appreciated the beauty of the San Francisco Bay Area. The Golden Gate Bridge symbolizes much of that beauty to me and brings back many happy memories." The quilt was based on a scenic photograph (pictured above) taken by Don Klosterman. She found the photograph as the result of an internet search on the web. "I Left My Heart" is a departure from Patty's traditional work and is the first quilt that she designed using the Picture Piecing technique. Details for the bridge cables were made with a combination of thread and permanent marker. The quilt took 3 weeks to complete and contains 714 pieces of fabric.

Photo 68A - Reference photograph.

Photo 68B - Sewn strawberries.

Shading

Three fabric shades are required for an object to appear real. Use light fabric to indicate highlights, medium fabric for the base color of the object, and dark fabric for shadows. If there is a fabric you want to emphasize, choose it as the medium shade. Medium shades are the most visible. For example, if you are designing an iris flower and have a beautiful purple fabric to showcase, make it the medium color in your flower. Shading highlights and shadows can also be accomplished with creative thread work and strategically placed quilting.

Lights and darks should contrast highly. If there is not much difference in the shades of fabric, the finished product appears washed out. When I made the wall hanging *Come Into the Light* (Page 6), I ran into this problem. The entire quilt was finished, and there was not enough contrast in lights and darks. To

remedy this problem, I added darker washes of paint and a significant amount of permanent marker rendering. Each spindle was outlined with a black marker and quilted in the ditch with black quilting thread to define them. See Chapter 6, Techniques, for more problem solving hints.

If you have doubts about whether fabrics are intense enough, it is best to lean toward the lighter shades. Light fabrics can be painted darker. It is more difficult to make a dark fabric lighter.

Use shading to define overlapping shapes. When two items are the same color, as these strawberries, in Photo 68A, you need definition between them. Place a dark fabric between the strawberries to differentiate between the two. If not, the two strawberries will run together and look like one blob of red fabric. Another way to prevent this prob-

Figure 68A - Begin by placing freezer paper over the line drawing.

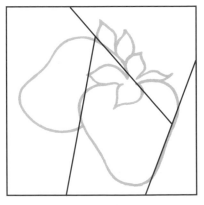

Figure 68B - The first sectioning lines are drawn.

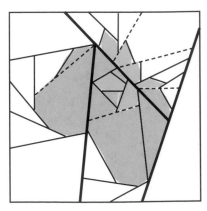

Figure 68C - Section the outside lines of the shape first.

lem is to introduce another shape or color between them. Do not forget to use the shading on the fabric itself to the best advantage. **Italic shade** notations (dk for dark) can be placed along the edges of the pattern as a reminder.

Add shadows and highlights to the design by shading areas that appear darkest in the photograph. Shade areas with a pencil or colored pencil, on the line drawing rather than on the freezer paper (Figure 69). Working from a photograph, you can see where the lights and darks are. Mark dark fabric notations first because they are easier to see. It may help to make a black and white photocopy of the photograph to determine where the darks are. Keep in mind where the light source would be and how objects are illuminated.

Use lines to section the outside edges of the strawberry. Then, further subdivide for shadows and highlights, working within the shapes previously sectioned. Extend lines out until you come to a previously drawn line. There are four **circle over an intersection** notations in this design due to shading (Figure 70C). When the pattern pieces are

Tip:

Remember to make basic outline divisions before shading.

sewn together, match these seams so that shading stays consistent.

Always make the basic outline divisions of a shape before adding shading. Do not add **circle placement numbers** until all sectioning is completed (including any shading divisions). As the pattern increases in complexity, the number of pattern pieces will increase. The more shading divisions, the more sewing is required, and the more realistic the design becomes.

Now that shading has been added to the design, the strawberry has three colors: a light red for the highlighted area, R1; a medium red, R2; and dark red, R3, for the shadow. Colors for the background and the leaves need to be noted. Mark **circle placement numbers, fabric color notations,** (Photo 70C) and **directional arrows** (if needed). Photocopy and sew.

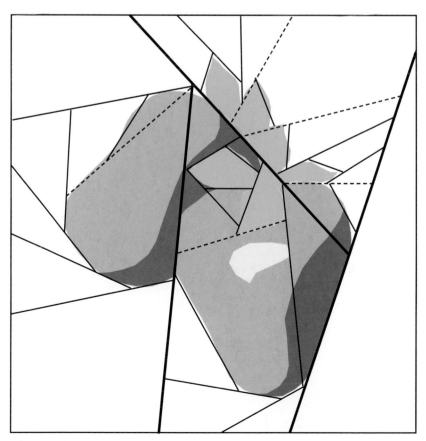

Figure 69 - Make all sectioning lines around the outline of the shape before concentrating on adding highlights and shadows. Indicate shading on the line drawing with a pencil or colored pencil.

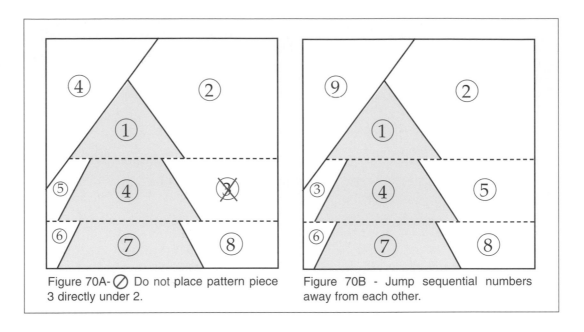

Figure 70A- ⊘ Do not place pattern piece 3 directly under 2.

Figure 70B - Jump sequential numbers away from each other.

Jumping the Numbers

Start numbering a section where two pattern pieces can be joined (a pair). Sometimes it is helpful to jump the sequential numbers away from one another to avoid confusion when sewing. For instance, in Figure 70A pattern pieces 1 and 2 are a pair and can be joined. If 3 is placed as in the figure you may try to sew it to 2 before the center subsection is complete. The **dotted line** indicates that the three subsections should be sewn separately and then joined. By placing 3 away from 2 it provides an additional reminder.

Rather than placing 3 directly under 2, start numbering with 3 to the far left of the center subsection (Figure 70B). This reinforces the idea that the three subsections need to be sewn together first, then joined.

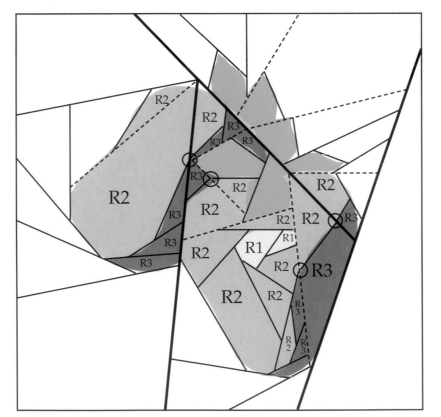

Figure 70C - Notice that adding lines to indicate shading means more **dotted lines**. There are now four **circle over an intersection** notations. The design now has three shades of red: R1, R2, and R3. Background **fabric color notations** and the green color notations would be added before photocopying. As you can see in the shaded illustration, division lines are made to indicate shapes rather than trying to replicate them exactly.

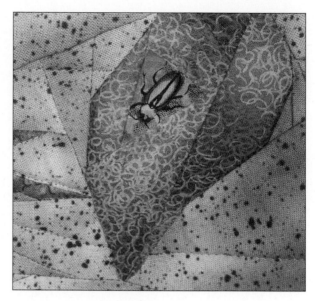

Photo 71A - Detail, *Blood, Sweat and Flowers*
Cynthia England
A conversation print with a white background was used to place this bug onto the lattice of the border.

Photo 71B - Detail, *Ambush*
Rhonda Gabriel
A green beetle was cleverly placed on a leaf in *Ambush*. Full view of quilt on Page 43.

Adding Conversation Prints

One of the biggest advantages to the Picture Piecing technique is the fact that construction is executed from the right side of the fabric. Extra sewing time is not required to add a little whimsey to your landscape, with the addition of conversation prints - a bug on a leaf, a hidden bunny. Children and adults alike love to find hidden objects within pictures. Some of us never grow up!

In this technique, pattern pieces are ironed directly on top of a fabric motif. Many of the quilts in this book contain conversation print motifs. The bug on the border of *Blood, Sweat and Flowers* (Page 47) was a printed conversation fabric that had a white background (Photo 71A). Rhonda Gabriel's stunning underwater scene, *Ambush* (Page 43), has a lime green beetle on the foliage (Figure 71B). *In the Southern Tradition* has a rabbit at the base of the large tree and two squirrels are hidden in the leaves (Photos 71C and 71D).

Photo 71C and 71D - Details, *In the Southern Tradition*
Cynthia England
Two different conversation prints were used in this quilt; a rabbit at the base of the tree and two squirrels are in the foliage. One of the squirrels is pictured in the detail, far right.

Photo 72A - Original photograph
In the Southern Tradition
This beautiful home is in League City, Texas, and was built in 1913.
Photograph by C. England.

Photo 72B - The back
In the Southern Tradition

Photo 72C - Line drawing. The most difficult aspect of the photograph was the porch railing. To simplify this, I left every other post out and made them straight.

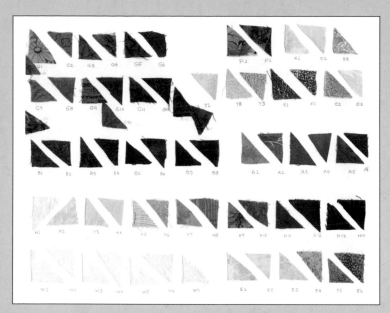

Photo 73A - The color chart

Photo 73B - *In the Southern Tradition*   1995   51" x 35"   Cynthia England
The inviting front porch became the inspiration for this wall hanging. The owners had painstakingly restored the home to its current splendor, and treated this artist to a wonderful tour of the interior; southern hospitality at its finest! Photograph by C.England.

Blending Conversation Prints

To achieve realism, try to choose conversation motifs that blend with surrounding fabrics. Fabrics such as these are relatively easy to camouflage (above). Light to medium shade backgrounds work best because the background fabric color can be modified with painting or markers to blend them in.

The swatches on Page 75 illustrate fabrics that may prove difficult to work with. Darker background fabrics attract more attention. Overlapping motifs can also cause concerns,

so avoid them. It is difficult to lighten a dark background. Of course, if the design is of a nighttime scene, dark fabric backgrounds may be appropriate. Fabrics with animals that have medium green backgrounds, and fabrics with insects on white or light blue backgrounds seem to work best.

If you know before beginning your project that you want to include a particular animal fabric, choose fabrics for that area that are similar in color. If the fabric is not in the

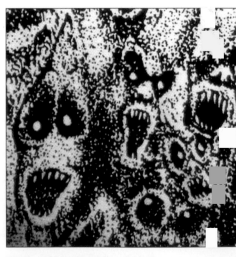

Photo 74A and 74B - Detail
Open Season
This creepy Halloween fabric was used throughout the quilt. When cut into small pattern pieces the faces disappear.
Photographs C. England.

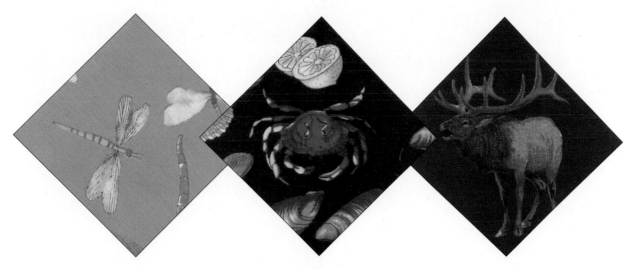

Problem Background Prints

desired color range, consider reversing it and then piecing the motif in, as in the deer in *Piece and Quiet* (Page 41). Color washes and marker rendering can be added to change the original fabric color.

I found a fun conversation print to add to my quilt *Open Season* (Page 61). I call it my "dead guy" fabric. It is covered with screaming, creepy, toothy monster faces (Photos 74A and 74B). The great thing about this fabric is that when it is cut into small pieces, it looks like a black and white texture and the faces disappear. Make the pattern pieces large enough and the faces are visible. There are three full faces in the quilt, but the fabric is used extensively throughout. Believe me, if you put a dead guy in a quilt, people will remember it! *Open Season* was finished in the year 2000, so I used a millennium conversation print fabric in the water with "2000" printed on it (Photo 75).

Photo 75 - Detail   *Open Season*
A millennium fabric that had "2000" printed on it was used in the water. Photograph C. England.

Photo 76A - Original photograph
Necia Wallace's dramatic photograph above is a reminder of the great times spent camping with her family.

Photo 76B - *Zion National Park*
2000   20" x 21"   Cynthia England

Placing the Motif

To use the butterfly print fabric pictured in Photo 77A, place freezer paper over the area of the fabric and draw an outline of the butterfly. Section out the base design of the leaf (Figure 76B). Decide where in the design you want to place the motif; in this case, the butterfly will be centered within the leaf shape (Figure 77A). Place the outline of the butterfly over the sectioned leaf to determine place

ment. With a pencil, draw in the pattern piece where the motif will be positioned.

Rarely will the conversation print fabric fit into the design precisely. The pattern pieces surrounding the conversation print must be adjusted to accommodate it. There are two ways to adjust the surrounding pattern pieces: decrease the size of the motif, or increase the size of the surrounding pattern pieces.

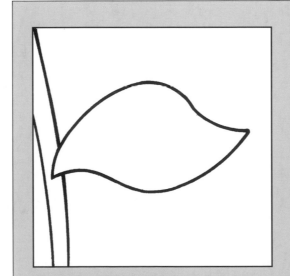

Figure 76A - Outline drawing of leaf.

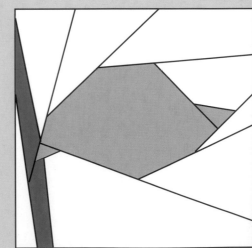

Figure 76B - Section out the leaf which the motif will be placed.

Photo 77A and 77B - Pictured above is the conversation print used in the pieced leaf at right.

Decreasing the Size of the Motif

This method decreases the size of the motif to accommodate the size of the pattern piece. Usually, more than one motif is printed in close proximity to another. In the example above, two butterflies are next to each other. If only one butterfly is desired, you can isolate a single object from the motif by decreasing the size to accommodate the pattern piece.

Isolate the fabric motif by placing additional sectioning lines along the outside edges of the butterfly. Work only within the pattern piece that was drawn (Figure 77B). It will look more natural if the fabrics used

around the butterfly are similar in color or painted to appear so. If possible, use parts of the same fabric that the conversation print came from. See Photo 77B for the finished sewn-in butterfly.

If you wanted to place this motif in a particular area of your pattern and the motif was too large, there is a way to change the surrounding pattern pieces to accommodate it.

Figure 77A - Place freezer paper over the fabric and outline the motif. Place it over the sectioned leaf to determine placement.

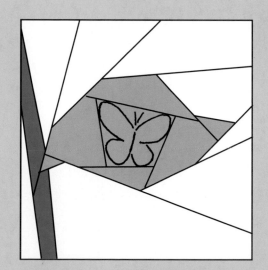

Figure 77B - To isolate the fabric motif further, place additional section lines along the edge of the butterfly. Work only within the original pattern piece.

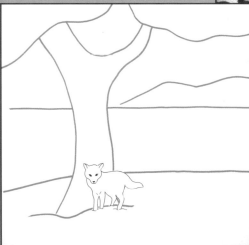

Figure 78A - Trace outline of motif.

Figure 78B - Decide where in the landscape to position the fox.

Figure 78C - When placing the fox consider the scale ot the tree.

Large Motifs

Along the bottom of the page, note the nice animal print. This print is wonderful and it has good contrast. The colors are realistic, and there are several animals to choose from. Pay particular attention to the fox near the top, right. He will be used to demonstrate how to work with large motifs, and will be placed in the landscape line drawing. Consider scale to determine where he would be best positioned. If he is placed too far forward in the design, he will not be big enough; too far back, and he will look like he could be ridden like a horse. The base of the tree would be a good choice.

Place freezer paper over the conversation print fabric and trace the outline of the fox (Figure 78A). Decide exactly where the fox will be positioned (Figure 78B, 78C). Section out the line drawing of the base design of the landscape (Figure 79A). Then, place the outline of the fox over the sectioned landscape, to see where the fox will be positioned. If the drawing is left as it was originally sectioned, there would be a line that cuts through the area where the fox would be (Figure 79B).

To avoid cutting through the fox, erase the set of division lines through him and under-

Photo 79 - Sewn in fox. The background around the fabric was painted to blend in.

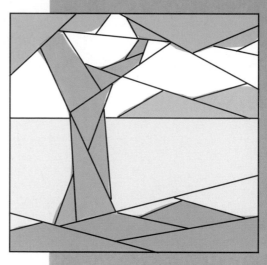

Figure 79A - Section out the landscape design.

neath the lower right side. Draw new pencil lines that will avoid intersecting the area. Isolate the fox motif by adding new lines around him (Figure 79C).

Numbering and **color notations** should be made **after** any changes are made to accommodate conversation prints motifs.

Figure 79B - Change the direction of the lines to avoid the fox.

Figure 79C - Change directions of new lines to isolate the fox.

Photos 80A and 80B
Dagger Flat   1996   44" x 61"   Carolyn Allison

The photograph to the left was taken during a family vacation at Big Bend National Park. Carolyn decided to try to recreate the rugged landscape. She added trapunto details to the yucca flower.
Carolyn said, "I didn't know if it would work or not, so I did the sky first which had bigger pieces. By the time I got to the top of the hills, I was pretty excited!"

Photo 81
Iris   1999   62" x 92"   Jo Fleming
Jo decided to combine her love of gardening with her love of quilting in this beautiful quilt. The quilt center is an enlarged picture pieced *Iris Beauty* pattern surrounded with incredible machine appliqued spring flowers.

Photo 82
Soli Deo Gloria (Glory to God Alone)
1995   36" x 36"   Patricia Pepe

Three of Cynthia England's pieced flower patterns, Hummingbird,
American Beauty and Wild Rose were manipulated to make this
beautiful quilt. A large scale floral fabric was used to create background roses. It was made for a quilt guild challenge, and it
received the Best of Show award.

Photo 83
The Wedding Quilt of Katie Caffrey and Scott Ferguson
1996   94" x 94"   Terri Caffrey

The center block of this medallion quilt is from a Picture Pieced pattern called
Wedding Bells. The block pattern used in the quilt is called Cake Stand. Each
block is 5" finished. Wedding guests signed the blocks and added good luck
wishes to commemorate the occasion.

Photo 84
Charleen's Roses   2000   63" x 63"   Jo Fleming

Cynthia England's *American Beauty* pattern was enlarged for the center of this stunning medallion quilt. Jo's machine appliqued roses surrounding the design set it off beautifully. Dark pink roses are her friend, Charleen's, favorite.

Photo 85
Roses are Red, Violets are Blue?   2002   50" x 64"
Norma DeHaven

This wall hanging was a significant departure into realism for the artist. She usually concentrates on more abstract pieces. A combination of Picture Piecing and curved piecing were used for this striking still life.

Photo 86A and 86B
Sunflowers   45" x 45"   2002   Katie Kelly
Katie's free use of color and texture add excitement to the Sunflower pattern. Notice the addition of the small pieced Ohio star blocks that are scattered throughout the background (detail at right).

Photo 87A
Heart & Palm 1997 11" x 12"
Peggy Timmons
Peggy decided to use the Picture Piecing technique for her Christmas exchange. This is one of twelve wall hangings that she designed and made. Her love of California explains the symbolism of the palm fronds and the heart.

Photo 87B - *Hummingbird with Indian Paintbrush* 1998 30" x 30" Leigh McDonald
A variety of hand-dyed fabrics were used to create this Jewel hummingbird. It is machine quilted in fantasy flower designs. Photograph by A. Daniel Messaros.

Chapter Six

Techniques

Y ou will come across many different situations when creating a pictorial quilt. Use your creativity to solve design problems. Each quilt is its own unique learning experience. With each new quilt, you will discover new techniques that work well for you. You will find that some techniques do not work so well. Do not be afraid to try something new. Remember, this is a *learning* experience.

A combination of techniques adds interest to the overall design of the quilt, just as different textures and fabrics add to the visual interest.

Decide at the onset of your project which aspects of your quilt might cause you some difficulty. Keep that in mind when choosing the technique that would get your idea across the best way.

Details can be executed in many different ways. If you do not want to machine piece it, then paint, applique, embroider, or embellish it. Remember, the end result is what matters - whatever works!

Photo 88 - Detail
The Power of Houston
Cynthia England
Libby Lehman
Vicki Mangum

The night sky literally sparkles with a variety of beautiful metallic quilting and decorative thread work. Full view of the quilt is on Page 91.

Photo 90
Source Graphic for *The Power of Houston*
This conceptual graphic was provided as the starting point for *Power of Houston.* It was created to celebrate "Sky Power & Beyond" which was sponsored by Reliant Energy - Power of Houston '99. An 8 1/2" x 11" color photocopy was provided to the quilt artists to use for reference purposes.
Conceptual graphic provided courtesy of JW Productions.

Photo 91
Power of Houston   1999   9' x 10'   Cynthia England, Libby Lehman, Vicki Mangum

This spectacular quilt depicts the skyline of Houston as it appeared during the millennium laser light show. The idea for this commemorative quilt came from Karey
Bresenhan of Quilts, Inc. The quilt was donated to the City of Houston, and is on display at the official Visitors Center. The quilt was made over a period of three months.
The artists met on two occasions to discuss design and fabric choices. Cynthia
England pieced the buildings in the lower half. Libby Lehman created the upper half,
and overlaid the fabulous fireworks. The two halves were made separately and joined
together at another meeting. Vicki Mangum added applique details, and made the quilt
sparkle with intricate metallic quilting.
Photograph by Jim Lincoln, courtesy of Quilts, Inc.

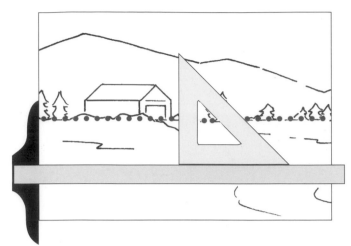

Figure 92
A T-square and drafting triangle will keep horizontal and vertical lines true. In the illustration at left, the horizon line (red dotted line) lines up with the horizontal line of the T-square. The side of the building aligns with the vertical line of the triangle.

Following are helpful tips on how to handle buildings, windows, trees, flowers, eyes, and clouds.

Altering the Fabric

To add painted details on the fabric, I use acrylic paints mixed with textile medium, thinned with water to create color washes for shading. Textile medium can be found at craft stores that sell painting supplies. It transforms acrylic paint into a washable fabric paint. Fabric dyes already have the textile medium mixed in. They can also be thinned with water and used as washes. I recommend painting with transparent washes because it is safer. If the paint is taken directly from the bottle, it will be intense in color; color washes allow you to add color gradually. Adding color is easy, while removing it, is not. After painting on the fabric, allow it to dry and then heat-set it with an iron.

Buildings

Generally, architectural designs are more difficult to work with than nature subjects. Seam lines must be straight, or the building or house leans. For example, in the wall hanging *In the Southern Tradition* (Page 73), there is a problem with the fourth white post from the left. It isn't straight, and bothers me every time I look at that quilt.

Think about investing in a T-square. It is a tool that artists and drafters use for alignment. It looks like what it is named after, the letter T. The short end of the T rests along the side of a straight edge (such as a table). It can be used alone by moving it up or down to obtain straight, parallel lines. If a plastic triangle is placed along the long end of the T, vertical lines can be obtained that are in square with the parallel lines. This tool will

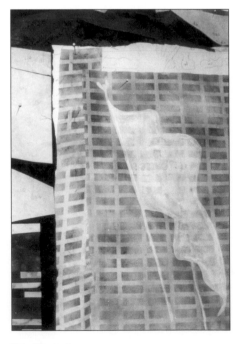

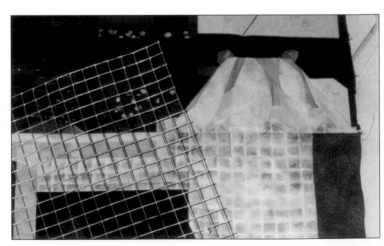

Photos 92A and 92B - Fabrics were stenciled to give the illusion of high rise structure and windows. Quilter's 1/4" tape was used to mask off this orange fabric to the left. Rabbit cage wire was stenciled over to create windows in the buildings. A white wash was painted behind the flag in preparation for the photo transfer. Photographs by C. England.

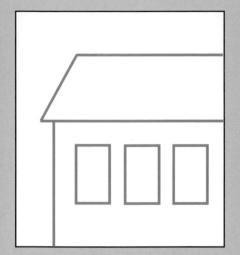

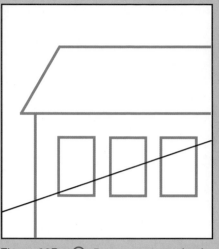

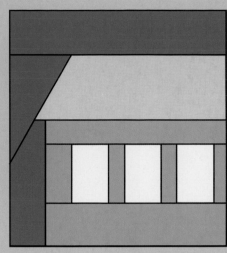

Figure 93A - Work around more than one window.

Figure 93B - ⊘ Do not cut randomly through windows.

Figure 93C - Make divisions along the top and bottom for easy sewing.

help keep building lines true. With a pencil, lightly draw in building lines on the freezer paper before placing sectioning lines over them. If layers accidentally shift while sectioning, the building lines will remain square.

In *The Power of Houston* quilt (Page 91), painted details were added to represent buildings (Photos 92A). On the building near the center, picturing Mount Rushmore, quilter's 1/4" tape was used to "stripe" the fabric, and then it was stenciled using a black wash.

Windows

One easy way to make window sashing is to let the fabric do the work for you. Find a fabric to represent them. Keep the scale of the window panes in mind; the light lines in a plaid may represent window sashing wood. Do not forget to check the backs of fabrics.

Windows were indicated in *The Power of Houston* by placing rabbit cage wire on top of the fabric and then lightly stenciling over it (Photo 92B).

If the window is large enough, piece it entirely, and add interest with a conversation print. Use a print that seems as if the viewer is looking out of the window into a scenic garden or a village (Photo 93).

In Figure 93A, there is a line drawing of a building with multiple windows. When sectioning windows, avoid cutting through them diagonally (Figure 93B).

Make the division lines on the pattern along the top and bottom of the windows. That way, there will be simple rectangles to sew together (Figure 93C).

Remember that you can also stencil or paint windows. In the wall hanging *Positano Italy Coastline* (Page 33), some of the windows were painted, and others were sewn by machine. Marker details were added after the piecing was completed. Windows were quilted to outline them, and to emphasize window sashing. When quilting, the painted windows were outlined, making it difficult to tell which were pieced and which were painted.

Photo 93 - A conversation print is used to suggest a scene outside the window.

Photo 94
Red Barn   2000   19" x 17"   Cynthia England

Trees

When trees are part of your design, try to make the sectioning lines vertical and diagonal. Before actually making any vertical divisions, try to separate the tree trunks from the ground and the foliage above (Figures 95A-95C). This keeps the foliage in the foreground and the tree behind it.

The first sectioning line in *Red Barn*, (Photo 94) was made from the top right edge of the tree trunk down to the bottom left hand corner of the tree trunk. Then, the line for the lower limb was drawn. This separates the tree from the rest of the picture.

Trees work well using gradual diagonal lines along the trunk (Figures 94A-94C). This is an excellent way to create movement throughout the tree. Not only does it help to move the viewer's eyes around, it also provides an opportunity for adding shadows and highlights (Figure 95D). Additional lines can be extended off of the diagonal line.

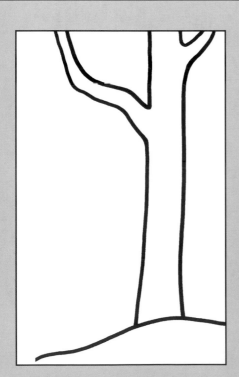

Figure 94A - Tree line drawing.

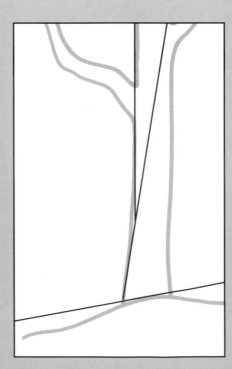

Figure 94B - Section trees diagonally rather than vertically.

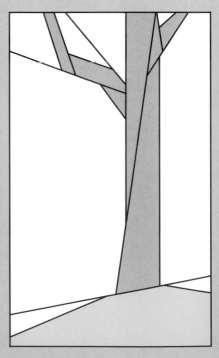

Figure 94C - Sectioned line drawing.

Figure 95A - Line drawing.

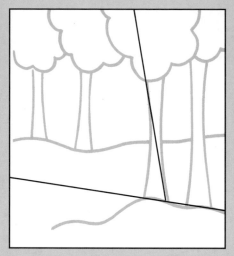

Figure 95B - Separate trees from the foreground first.

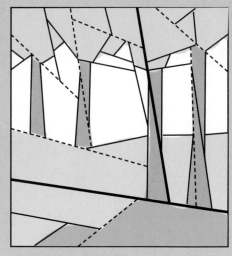

Figure 95C - Section the foliage next.

Bushes and Flowers

Find representational fabrics to indicate bushes and flowers. If there is a field of flowers, consider choosing a few of the more prominent ones and drawing attention to them. Use applique to place them on top of the pieced background, or sew them in the same way as you would the rest of the design. Applique does offer one advantage, an extra layer of batting can be placed between the quilt top and the batting to make the flowers stand out a bit.

In *Split Rail* (Page 37), I needed a daisy fabric with a dark green background for the flowers in the front. I did manage to locate a daisy print with a white background. The fabric was pieced in with the white background, and the color changed to a dark one with a combination of paint and permanent marker (Page 34).

Figure 95D - This method provides an opportunity for shading the tree.

Tip:

Freezer paper makes an excellent disposable painting palette. Turn the freezer paper shiny side up and mix the paints directly on it.

Also, freezer paper can be ironed onto the back of the fabric on which you are painting. It will stabilize the fabric and keep any paint from seeping through.

Figure 96A

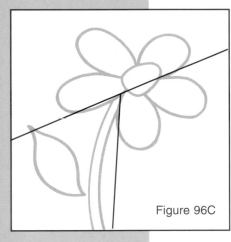

Figure 96B

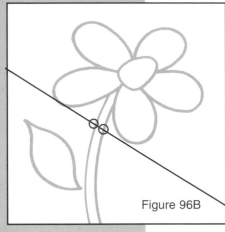

Figure 96C

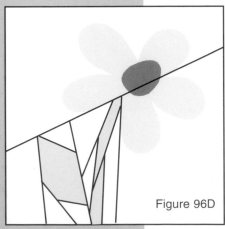

Figure 96D

Be careful when sectioning flower stems (Figure 96A). Watch out for those **circle over an intersection** notations. Do not cut directly through a stem if you can avoid it (Figure 96B). Work around the problem area first. This is similar to the way a tree trunk is handled; try to separate the stem from the flower above. By doing this first, other lines will be created to work from (Figure 96C). It is better to make the division to the side of the stem rather than cut through it (Figure 96D). This hint works well for narrow objects that require matching points if cut across **circle over an intersection** notations. Sometimes circle matches are necessary; however, if they can be avoided, all the better!

Clouds

Frequently the question arises, "I have a landscape that has a large area of sky. Should I make this one large piece of fabric, or break it apart?" (Figure 97B). This is a personal decision. If there is a fabulous, hand-dyed fabric that looks exactly like your vision of the sky, then use it. Patty Dillon used one beautiful sky fabric in her quilt, *I Left My Heart* (Page 67). Sometimes, however, a pattern piece that is much larger than all the others will look out of place. *Piece and Quiet* (Page 9) has one

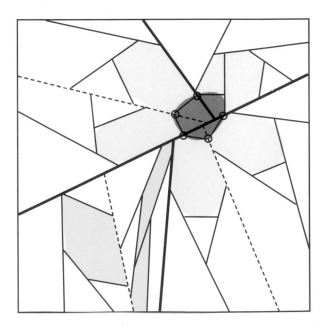

Figure 96E - Completed sectioned flower.

large rock in the stream near the center. I felt that one piece of fabric in the midst of an intricate pieced river would appear awkward, so I subdivided the rock as well.

Sky can be subdivided by adding curved lines on the line drawing to indicate clouds (Figure 97C). If a very subtle look is desired, choose fabric shades that are close in value. If you would rather have puffy, white clouds, use a bright white for the highlight areas and a medium blue for shadows. Find other photographs of clouds for drawing and color reference.

Sectioning cloud shapes requires dealing with curves. The first line is placed along the edge of one of the curves. Draw it from top to bottom (Figure 97D). Then, pull lines out from it to complete the sectioning of the design (Figure 97E). This method is very similar to Indicating Movement (Page 59) for thickening tree limbs. After the lines are sectioned, drop down below the original drawn line and make a new set of lines (Figure 97A). This new set of lines allows the pattern pieces above to be marked with a different fabric color, such as white highlights. Lines can also be placed below to indicate another fabric color for shadows.

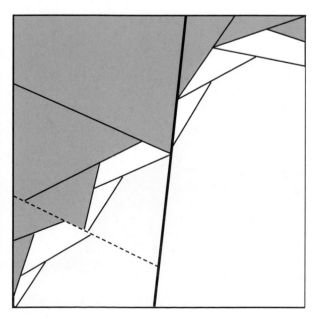

Figure 97A - Additional sectioning lines were added to allow for shading.

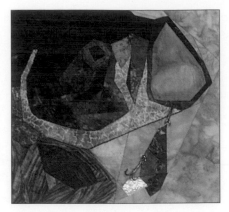

Photo 98A and 98B - *Tony's Fish*
2001   31" x 32"   Nancy Pocklington
Nancy's first attempt at designing her own pattern was made for her husband, an avid bass fisherman. There are real hooks on the lure.

Photo 98C
Woodland Morning   2001   40" x 30"   Eunice M. Hill
Eunice captured the morning light streaming through the trees with her careful selection of fabrics. She worked from several photographs of the area and added appliqued wildlife details. Photograph by Warner Halverson.

Photo 99 - *Meadow Run Dreams*   2001   28" x 44"   Eunice M. Hill
A scenic area of Minnesota was recreated in fabric by Eunice Hill. She hiked the bluff
to take pictures to capture the feeling of the area. There is a dog hidden in the stream
bank area. Private Collection. Photograph by Warner Halverson.

Photo 100 - *Tall Timbers Tranquility*   1998   62" x 90"   Eunice M. Hill
This quilt depicts a northern Wisconsin Lake and its wildlife. There are animals throughout the quilt: a deer, fox, and two bear. The totem design on the right border is a piece of folk art on the owner's property. Private Collection. Photograph by Warner Halverson.

Photos 101A and 101B
Waiting for Inspiration
2002   73" x 60"
Nan Moore

This intriguing quilt (below) pulls the viewer through the gate and into the garden. Nan has used a variety of fabrics and included some surprises in the foliage. At right, are just a couple of the creatures that are pieced in. Seated just beyond the gate is a person "waiting for inspiration."

Photo 102
Memories of Italy   1994   43" x 43"   Dorothy Smith

Dorothy and her family sponsored an Italian foreign exchange student and years later visited him in Italy. She wanted to capture the warmth and light from the villages that she recalled from this memorable vacation. A painting by Gustav Klimt provided the visual inspiration for this piece. Photograph by Kabe Russell.

Photo 103A - *Pride of Nebraska* 2001 98" x 72" Janice Lippincott

This landscape depicts a rural area in Nebraska extending from the Missouri River near Blair, westward ten miles to Arlington, along the Elkhorn River. This quilt was a commission piece made for Two Rivers Bank which has locations in each of these two towns. Photograph by Michael Dwyer.

Photo 103B - *Jordan Baptism* 1998 76" x 38" Rosemary Cochran England

This altar cloth was made for St. Stephen's Episcopal Church in Terre Haute, Indiana. Rosemary depicted the baptism of Christ in the Jordan River. The water swirl symbolizes the event, and the dove, the Holy Spirit descending. Photograph by Adrian Taylor.

Photo 104A
This beautiful house surround-
ed by bluebonnets is in
Jefferson, Texas. It appeared in
the *Texas Magazine* of *The
Houston Chronicle.*

Photo: Houston Chronicle by E.
Joseph Deering ©2000 Houston
Chronicle Publishing Co. Re-
printed with permission. All
Rights Reserved.

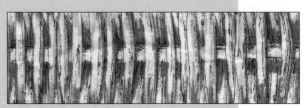

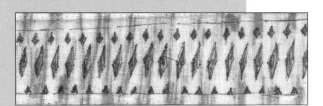

Photos 104B and 104C
The porch railing on *Bluebonnet Hill*
started from a basket weave patterned
fabric. In the detail at the top you can
see how the front of the fabric looked.
The back of the fabric was altered with
a permanent marker to create the illusion of porch railing (above).
Photographs by C. England.

Photos 104D and 104E - *Bluebonnet Hill*
(right) has three different scale bluebonnet fabrics in it. The largest one has white
flowers sprinkled in among the blue (top,
left). When the wall hanging was finished,
the white flowers were distracting. To
blend them in, I painted them with a blue
wash (above).

Photo 105
Bluebonnet Hill   2002   33" x 35"
Jerryann Corbin and Cynthia England

Trees were rearranged and eliminated from the original photograph, and the chimney omitted. Two native Texans collaborated to make this charming quilt.

Photo 106A and 106B
Influences II: Gauguin
2001   21" x 26"
Norma DeHaven

This quilt depicts a self-portrait of Gauguin, and is the second in a series of tributes to artists who have influenced Norma's life. Masterful use of color, and clever detailing of the fringed moustache (detail), combine to create this striking portrait.

Faces

Some quilt artists choose to machine piece features, others opt to paint the features after piecing. Still, others applique the face. Norma DeHaven suggests trying to find a number of flesh tones with subtle differences in color, for shadows and highlights. The pieced face in her quilt, *Tribute to Gauguin,* (Photos 106A and 106B) makes use of a wonderful variety of prints and textures. To add interest in the piece she even fringed the mustache. Another excellent example are the faces of the jazz musicians in her quilt, *Jazzers,* on Page 122.

Take into consideration the age of the subject being portrayed. Older faces provide excellent opportunities for shading due to wrinkles and age lines. Children may look best with a limited amount of sectioning and use of softer fabrics. Do not forget to check fabric backs.

In *Best Friends* (Photo 107B), colors were created by using a muslin fabric and painting transparent washes from light to dark. Fabric swatches were then cut from the different areas to create various flesh tones.

When shopping for flesh tones, remember to look at only one layer of the fabric. Layer upon layer of flesh-colored fabric on a bolt will appear brighter than it actually is.

Photos 107A and 107B
Best Friends 1997 18" x 24"
Cynthia England

Original 3" x 5" photograph used for *Best Friends,* taken
by the author.

This wall hanging (below) was part of a traveling exhib-
it of fifty quilts. Each artist was asked to make a quilt
18" x 24" representing a "Kiss." This quilt depicts my
daughter, Monica, kissing our dog, Maggie. We found
Maggie at the Humane Society. She is part Chihuahua
and part Pekingese, and weighs approximately thir-
teen pounds. The two of them have a very special
relationship.

Use Basic Embroidery Stitches to Add Detail

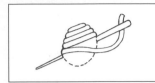

Stem Stitch - Work from left to right. Take even, slightly slanted stitches along the line. The needle comes out on the left side of the previous stitch.

Satin Stitch - Straight stitch across the shape, taking care to place the threads very close together.

Double-Padded Satin Stitch - Fill the shape with a satin stitch. Then, cover it by placing stitches horizontally.

Eyes and Embroidered Details

Avoid sectioning through eyes when making divisions. This will create **circle over the intersection** notations and will be distracting. Make division lines to the side.

Think of eyes in terms of oval or round shapes (Figure 109A). Section them as a curve (Page 55). Make the division lines above the eye, then extend lines out as in Figure 109B. If the division lines are placed very close together to form an exact replica of the line drawing, sewing will be difficult and many seams can be distracting. Make the lines farther apart, as in the illustration. The eyes can be defined further using a black, fine-lined permanent marker to round the edges. Block in those areas with the marker.

Photo 108A - Detail
Great Horned Owl
1999 Cynthia England

Photo 108B
Detail of *Quilter's Kitty*
1998 Cynthia England

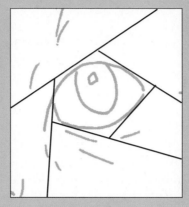

Figure 109A
Line drawing of cat's face.

Figure 109B
Remember not to cut through the center of the eye.

Figure 109C
Use a permanent, fine-lined marker to color in corners to indicate a curve.

This will make the eyes look more realistic (Figure 109C).

Depending on the size, it may be more practical to use surface embellishment for eye details rather than deal with intricate piecing. A two-strand embroidery Satin Stitch (Page 108) can be used to fill in an eye shape, then a highlight added with white thread.

The eagle's eye and talons in *Land That I Love* (Page 112) were achieved with embroidery. When the wall hanging was completed, the white of the eagle's head and the light gray tail feathers did not show up against the light blue background. A two-strand black Stem Stitch solved this contrast problem.

Embroidery details were added to *Lily Pond* by using a Double-Padded Satin Stitch to increase visibility (not for the frog, for the viewer) (Page 110). A permanent marker was used to render the outside of this frog eye. The mouth line is a two strand Stem Stitch.

Poinsettia Basket, on Page 130, uses a stem stitch to connect the small leaf fronds rather than trying to piece the tiny stems.

Using Photo Transfers

Photo transfers can be used to create interest on the quilt surface. Images can be pieced into the quilt just as in the method used for conversation prints on Page 71. You may want to commemorate a special occasion, such as the wedding photo in *Treasured Memories* (Photo 111C). Or, perhaps you wish to include a photo of a family pet in your quilt. The possibilities are endless.

Wendy Foist used photo transfers of the rescue workers in her quilt *Unlimited Courage, Unlimited Love* (Page 112) as a remembrance of the September 11th tragedy.

Photo transfers were used in *The Power of Houston* (Page 91), for the images of the astronaut, Mount Rushmore, and the flags on the buildings. When the photo transfers were initially ironed to the fabric, there was not enough contrast. To remedy this, I decided to first paint the building fabric with a white wash in the areas where the photo transfers were to be placed. Photos 111A and 111B show the difference the background wash made, especially in the faces. Photo transfers were then ironed to the fabric after the building fabric was altered. When transferring photographs, the image will come out in reverse. Make a mirror image color copy to eliminate this problem. Mount Rushmore was almost sewn in backwards!

You can make your own photo transfers using an inkjet printer and textile heat transfer paper. Personally, I think, it is worth the money to have the image made and ironed on to my fabric by a company that specializes in that process. Temperature, and applying the right amount of pressure are very important when ironing the transfer on.

Photos 110A and 110B
Lily Pond   1998
Cynthia England   17" x 17"

The frog's eye uses a combination of embroidery and marker rendering.

Smearing can be another concern when applying the transfer yourself.

However, if you are planning to have many transfers in your project, it may be cost prohibitive and a good idea to do it yourself. For more information about companies that can provide this service and the supplies to do it yourself, see the Source Listing on Page 132.

Photos 111A and 111B - Detail
Power of Houston
The fabric was prepared with an opaque white wash to make the photo transfers show up on the mauve fabric.

Photo 111C - *Treasured Memories*
1999   20" x 20"   Cynthia England
A photo transfer was used for the picture on the table.

Photo 112A
Land That I Love   2001   27" x 27"
Cynthia England

I was proud of the way our citizens united and helped one another throughout the September 11th disaster. This quilt is a reflection of the patriotism sweeping the country.

Photo 112B - Below
Unlimited Courage, Unlimited Love
2001   63" x 73"
Pieced by Wendy Foist, Quilted by Kathy Olson

This quilt is dedicated to the rescuers and the strength of America. The quilt design is based on a 2" photo of the ruins. The background is Picture Pieced, and the top is embellished with embroidery and photo transfers.

Photos 113A and 113B
Detail - *Our Katy Remembered*
1996   58" x 42"
Suzanne Muse Taylor

This heart warming quilt was made for Suzanne's son when his cat was hit by a car. The photograph to the left was used for reference.
Original photograph taken by Suzanne Muse Taylor.

Chapter Six

Finishing

Decisions, decisions...when it comes to finishing your quilt there are a multitude of choices. Some quilters like to plan borders before beginning; other quilters wait and let the quilt top "speak" to them when it is finished.

For a realistic look, you may choose to add borders that look like a framed painting. A small inner accent border can represent an inner picture mat and a larger outside border can represent a picture frame.

The border should compliment the piece without distracting from the main interest of the design. The design can continue out over the border, even over the binding.

If your quilt is busy, consider a simple border solution. Perhaps a creative binding is all the quilt needs. A narrow inner border, or possibly one outside border may be all that is needed. There is no written rule that says you must have four borders. It is your quilt. You get to decide.

This chapter offers ideas on how to put the finishing touches on your quilt, from borders to binding.

Photo 114 - Detail
Bluebonnet Hill
2002   33" x 35"
Jerryann Corbin
Cynthia England

Details on the porch railing were made with markers and paint. The source photo was taken from a newspaper. Full view of the quilt is on Page 105.

Squaring The Quilt

First impressions make a difference when displaying a pictorial quilt. It should hang straight and flat. One **big** advantage in making a pictorial quilt is that size is usually not a determining factor. If a pictorial quilt is long on one side, it can be trimmed.

The finished quilt will need raw edges straightened. Here are a few methods for obtaining that "professional" look:

- Horizon lines are the basis to use for squaring a pictorial quilt (Photo 92). Find the horizon line, and move the T-square to the top or bottom to determine where the first line should be marked.
- Decide which part of the quilt you are willing to sacrifice. Slivers from the edges must be cut away. Usually, one portion of the quilt will contain more intricate piecing.
- Use a colored pencil to mark this line.
- Trim off this marked edge with a rotary cutter and ruler while maintaining as much of the edge as possible.
- After the first cut line is determined, move the T-square around and repeat the process for the other three sides.

Photo 116B
Twill tape is a great way to stabilize the edges of your quilt top. It will not stretch and helps to keep the quilt top square.

Stabilizing the Edges

Picture Piecing produces many, many seams. To keep seams from unraveling along outer edges, sew a long basting stitch with a walking foot attachment. Sew slightly less than 1/4" from the edge. This prevents stretching and unraveling. This basting seam will be covered when the binding is attached.

Twill Tape

The more seams, the heavier the quilt. The heavier the quilt, the more stabilization it requires to keep it from stretching because of the extra weight. Twill tape is a wonderful, inexpensive way to strengthen the outside edges of the quilt. It is lightweight, colorfast, and made for reinforcement purposes. I prefer to mark placement lines on the quilt, and then sew the twill tape on. Before trimming, double check that the quilt is still square.

To determine the amount of twill tape required, measure the circumference of the quilt. Twill tape can be purchased in 1/8" and 1/4" widths; however, I think for stabilizing the 1/4" width is best.

Twill tape can be found at general fabric stores and is available in a variety of colors. It is typically located near the packaged bindings. The tape is sewn on the edge of the quilt and will be placed under the binding, so it should not show. Choose a color similar to the edges of the quilt.

Photo 116A
Victorian Heart   1994   20" x 20"   Cynthia England

Photos 117A and 117B
Teton Mountains
1995   26" x 36"   Cynthia England
Pictured to the right is the original line drawing for the *Teton Mountains* pattern. Only two black inner borders are in this quilt (below, right).

Measure the top, center, and bottom of the quilt. Use the average measurement, and cut two pieces of twill tape the same size. Pin each end to the quilt first, and then place a pin in the center. Add additional pins about every five inches. Be careful not to stretch the quilt (Photo 116B). Use a normal stitch length, and a walking foot to sew down the center of the twill tape. Repeat for the other sides.

Border Treatments

Teton Mountains has a black inner border on two sides (Photos 117A and 117B). The large dark tree to the left provided the balance needed for the design. Whatever the preference, here are some good ideas for border and binding treatments.

Eunice Hill's creative border decision in the narrow inner border of her quilt *Tall Timbers Tranquility* (Page 100) is fabulous. Subtle color variations add interest while maintaining the restful feel of the piece. An accent border of this nature must be designed into the quilt initially. Border treatments with overlapping objects also require planning before sewing begins.

Janice Lippincott chose to add a narrow border for *Pride of Nebraska* (Page 103), and repeat colors across the horizon line. Note that the border along the top was eliminated. In this case, it softens the sky. The sky was sectioned in the direction that the clouds were moving. In the foreground, diagonal divisions bring the eye to the center of the quilt.

Applique can enhance the border as well. Jo Fleming chose to applique a wreath of roses around the central design in her quilt *Iris* (Page 81). A variety of traditionally pieced borders frame the outside edges. Notice the use of the tiny gold accent border.

Hang your quilt on the design wall and "audition" different fabrics to see what best sets off your design.

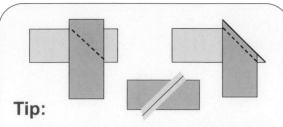

Tip:

When seaming either a border or a binding, join the seam with a 45-degree angle. It will lay flat and look more professional. Press the seam open.

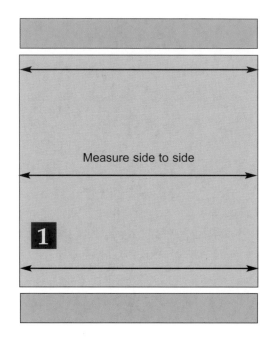

Measure side to side

1

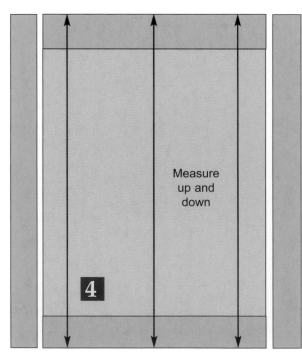

Measure up and down

4

After your finished quilt top is squared with a rotary mat and cutter, it is time to add the borders.

There are two basic border techniques that are commonly used to finish a quilt: one is a square cut corner border, and the other is a mitered corner.

Square Cut Corners

The square cut corner border is the fastest and easiest of the two. The top and bottom borders will be joined to the quilt top first, then the sides are attached. All seams must be sewn with a 1/4" seam (no paper moving here!).

To make a square cut corner border, begin by measuring your quilt.

1 Measure the width of the quilt top from side to side, horizontally. Take a measurement from both sides, and again, down the center. Take the *average* of the three for the final measurement. No matter how careful you were when the quilt top was constructed there will probably will be some variance in these measurements.

2 Cut border strips the width of the border desired, and seam them to the correct length.

3 Sew a border strip to the top and bottom of the quilt top. Press seam toward border.

4 Repeat the process in Step one above; this time measuring the quilt vertically.

5 Cut border strips the desired width, and seam to the vertical measurement. Sew to the sides of the quilt top. Press.

5

Mitered Corners

Mitered corners are the second most common way of finishing a border. A mitered corner looks more like the way a picture is framed.

If you have more than one border, a small inner border and a larger outside border, sew the two together before mitering.

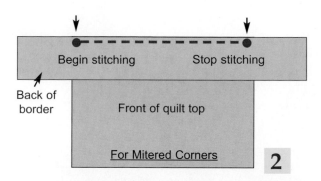

Begin stitching   Stop stitching

Back of border

Front of quilt top

For Mitered Corners

2

1 Estimate the finished outside dimensions of the quilt, including borders. When cutting your borders for mitering, add an extra 3 inches beyond your measurement, but do not cut anything to size yet.

2 Center the border strip on the quilt top edge and begin stitching 1/4" from the left quilt top edge, to 1/4" from the right quilt top edge. Backstitch to secure. Press toward the border.

3 Do the same on the other sides.

4 Face the quilt top, right side up on a flat surface. Bring the right side up at a 45-degree angle and align the border edges. Check to make sure that the seams line up on both borders.

5 Place a quilter's ruler along the fold, and use a pencil to mark a line. Pin the borders together and stitch this line. Backstitch to secure. Do not cut anything at this point.

6 Open up the top, and check to see that seams align (especially if you have more than one border to miter). If they do, then use the quilter's ruler and cut 1/4" past the sewn seam. If not, make adjustments to the seam.

7 Follow the same process for the other three corners. Iron the seam open.

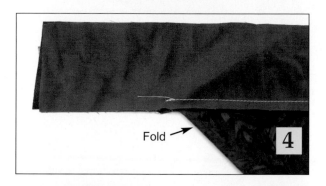

Fold

4

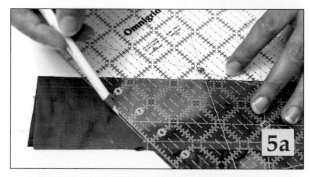

5a

5b

7

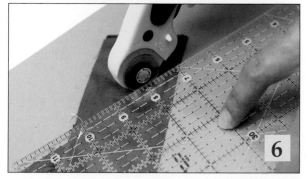

6

Photo 120 - Detail
Open Season (back)
Cynthia England

Backing

Consider using more than one fabric for the back of the quilt. It is an economical way to use leftover fabric from the quilt top. I prefer not to plan intricate designs for the back. Try to relate the design of the quilt backing to the design of the front. The back of *Come Into the Light* (Photo 121A) depicts a keyhole in the right corner and several skeleton keys floating in the foreground. This associates the idea of the entry door on the front. When my grandfather passed away, I was able to obtain some of the skeleton keys from his house. The keys were outlined, enlarged, and then appliqued to the back. The shadows under the keys are made with a permanent marker.

The imagery on the back of *Open Season* (Photo 121B) represents a stylized forest. A bright red cardinal was pieced into the back as my way of saying "enough of these monochromatic colors!" It expresses my joy in finishing a project that spanned six years.

The inspiration for your quilt can be reflected on the back with a photo transfer. *In the Southern Tradition* (Page 73), uses two photo transfers on the back: one of the house, and another for the foreground flowers.

Make sure to use good quality fabric on the back of the quilt. The backing should extend at least 2 inches around the outside dimensions of your finished top.

The top is completed, the backing is finished, now place batting between the layers.

Batting

Many different types of batting are available on the market: cotton, polyester, wool, poly/cotton, and endless varieties of those mentioned. Choose high-quality batting. Inexpensive batting may have migrating fibers that sometimes beard through the layers. Pictorial quilts are not made for warmth, they are made to display. A thin, lightweight batting that retains its shape is the primary concern. Choose a batting that can be stitched at least 5 inches apart to allow flexibility in the choice of quilting designs. Battings are now available in white, natural and black. Read the manufacturers label. See the Source listing (Page 132) for recommendations.

I prefer cotton batting, but used polyester batting in *Open Season* (Page 61). It is an extremely heavy quilt. Polyester and wool

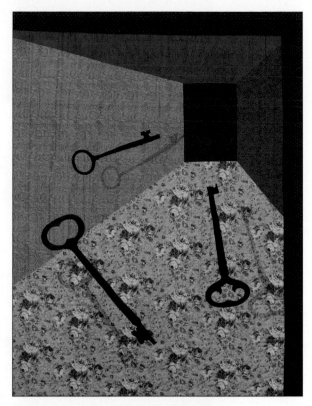

Photo 121A - *Come Into the Light* (back)
1992   43" x 64"   Cynthia England
Skeleton keys were appliqued on the back of the quilt
to tie in with the entry way door on the front (Page 6).

batting are known for shape retention.

Either hand-baste or use safety pins to hold the layers together during quilting.

Quilting Decisions

Look closely at the photographs that were referred to as your quilt was made. They will give hints as to how the quilt could be quilted. Look for waves in water, wind in the sky, siding on houses, and petals on flowers. As with seam lines, quilting lines pull the eye throughout the quilt.

This method does not lend itself to hand quilting. There are too many seam lines. When machine quilting, I recommend using a monofilament thread on top, and a cotton thread in the bobbin that matches the backing. Quilt in the ditch around the main objects of the design; add definition as needed. There is no need to outline every shape. For marking quilting lines, I like to use a #2 lead pencil on light fabrics. For darker fabrics, I use colored pencils; specifically white, silver, and yellow. I find that they adhere to the fabric a bit longer than others. Use a light touch when marking.

Photo 121B - *Open Season* (back)
2000   87" x 90"   Cynthia England
Front view of quilt is on Page 61. Photograph
by Mellisa Karlin Mahoney, courtesy of *Quilter's Newsletter Magazine.*

Finishing • 121

Photos 122A and 122B - *Jazzers*
2002   47" x 52"   Norma DeHaven
Created for the "Celebrate Diversity" theme at the Rocky Mountain Quilt Museum, this quilt represents, loosely, "The Duke" Ellington (piano), John Coltrane (sax), and Norma's son, John, on trumpet. The clever border pulls your eye in and throughout the design.

Binding

Binding provides the final frame for your quilt. There are choices to make when considering the type of binding that best suits the design. Scalloped or curved edges will require a bias binding. Following are directions for making straight of grain binding, and a special picture extended binding. Be sure to avoid stretching the quilt top.

Straight of Grain Binding

Square or rectangular quilts can use a straight of grain binding. Directions to the right are for a single-color, folded, double binding.

I like a narrow binding and cut my strips 2 1/4" wide. Binding cut this size will finish about 3/8" wide. To begin, measure the quilt's outside edges and add about eight or nine inches to the total. For example, if your quilt is 60" x 80", you need 289" of binding. Cut the appropriate number of strips, and join them with a 45-degree angle, as shown on Page 118. Join all strips together in this manner to make one long, continuous strip. Fold the entire strip of binding with wrong sides together, lengthwise; press.

After squaring the quilt and stabilizing the edges, determine if you will do part of the binding by hand or all by machine. Traditionally, binding is sewn to the front of the quilt and then turned to the back, and slip stitched to secure it. This gives a nice, professional finish. There is another way to attach the binding. It can be sewn initially to the back of the quilt and then turned to the front, and machine stitched. This is a good way to finish utilitarian quilts. After all, if the quilt is entirely machine made, why go to the trouble of using handwork to bind it?

Place binding on the front or back of the quilt accordingly, matching raw edges of binding to raw edges of quilt. Start binding about midpoint on one side of the quilt. Do not start too close to a corner, because the seam lines (that join the strips of binding) can cause a problem if they fall in a corner.

Fold →

1 Begin sewing about eight inches from the end of the binding. Backstitch to secure the thread, and sew 1/4" from the raw edge. Continue sewing until 1/4" from the corner of the quilt. Stop sewing, and backstitch.

2 Fold the binding up at a 45-degree angle.

3 Then, fold it down on the angle that you just made, lining up the edge of the binding with the next side of the quilt. Hold the fold down so it lays flat. This extra fabric is needed for a neat corner when the binding is stitched down.

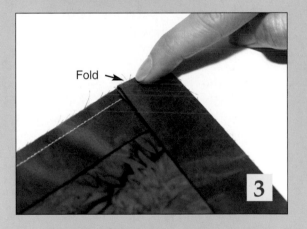

4 Sew beginning at the folded edge and backstitch to secure threads. Sew to the next corner, and repeat the process. Stitch all four corners in the same manner. When you get about ten to twelve inches from where the binding was originally sewn, stop and backstitch.

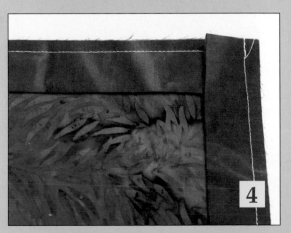

Final Seam for Binding

Now, to join the final seam. The final seam must be cut and joined at 45-degree angles. If it is joined with a straight seam it will contain excess fabric and appear lumpy. For professional results, lay the quilt on a flat surface.

1 Open the lower binding strip and cut off a 45-degree angle.

2 Place the lower binding strip along the edge of the quilt and insert a straight pin, horizontally, 1/2" from top of the cut angle.

3 Then, lay the top binding strip over the lower one. Place another straight pin through the *bottom layer* of the binding that is on top. Use the original pin as a guide for placement.

4 The second pin inserted becomes the marking place for cutting the 45-degree angle in the top binding strip.

5 Open the top binding and cut at a 45-degree angle using the pin as a starting point. **Both 45-degree cuts must be made in the same direction**. Remove the pin before cutting this angle.

6 Join the two binding ends as shown. Place the joined binding along the edge of quilt, and sew it to the quilt. Complete the binding by slip-stitching it on the back.

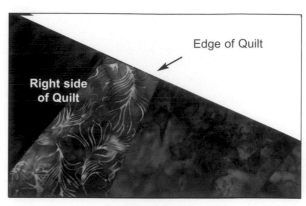

Photo 124 - Lay a strip of freezer paper (shiny side down) along the edge of the quilt.

Picture Extended Binding

Open Season (Page 61) is a *big* quilt. It is so big, in fact, that there was not room to add a border. If the size was increased even two inches, the quilt would no longer fit on the wall in my studio. Although I have nothing against large quilts, I had visions of moving to another house in the future where I could not hang the quilt. For that reason, I decided to add an interesting binding. I chose to extend the quilt design to the outside edges of the binding. I had never tried this before, and was a little apprehensive. After playing with folded paper, I decided to machine piece the binding using the Picture Piecing technique, then sew it on traditionally. To my delight (and relief), it worked beautifully. Following are directions on how to jazz up a quilt with pieced binding.

Lay the squared and stabilized quilt on a

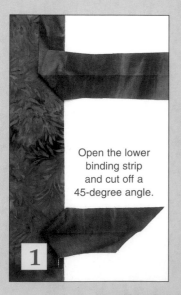

Open the lower binding strip and cut off a 45-degree angle.

1

Place pin 1/2" from top of angle

Omnigrid

2

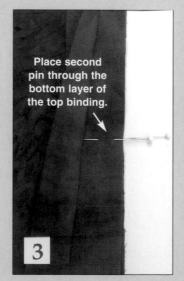

Place second pin through the bottom layer of the top binding.

3

Use the second pin as a cutting guide for the upper binding.

4

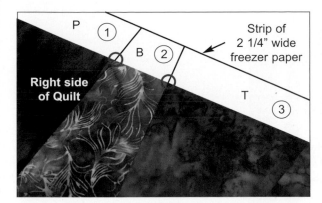

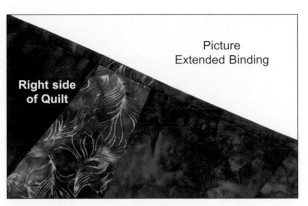

Photo 125A - Use a pencil and straight edge to extend lines straight out from desired areas of the quilt. Fold and sew on the binding. Match the seams at circle over the intersection marks.

Photo 125B - The finished Picture Extended binding continues the design over the edges of the quilt.

flat surface, such as a table. Determine the size that the finished binding will be. I usually cut mine 2 1/4" wide. Cut strips of freezer paper the same width. Tape enough strips together to equal the length of one side of the quilt. Tape the strips together as discussed on Page 51. Lay the freezer paper strip, with the paper side up and shiny side down, along the edge of the quilt. Determine which lines to extend. Every seam line does not need to be extended. Choose the most noticeable color changes.

I decided in *Open Season* that main branch lines and noticeable color changes would be placed over the binding. For example, when sectioning a snowy area, white fabrics were used; in areas that had many grays and whites, fabrics were chosen that contained a combination of both of these colors. Blending colors in intricate pieced areas will require less sewing.

Keeping the freezer paper along the edge of the quilt (it might be a good idea to tape it lightly), use a pencil and a straight edge to extend lines across the freezer paper. (Photo 125A). When the binding is sewn onto the quilt, make sure to treat these extended lines as matching points (**circle over an intersection** notations). Match points in the illustration are indicated by red circles. Align and pin these seams when sewing. Add **circled placement numbers** and fabric **color notations**. Photocopy the strip of freezer paper. Cut it up, and use the photocopy as the master. Sew the binding on traditionally, and slip-stitch it to the quilt back.

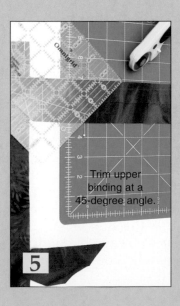

Trim upper binding at a 45-degree angle.

5

Join ends with a 1/4" seam allowance.

6a

Binding will lay flat along the quilt.

6b

Turn the binding to the back of the quilt and slip stitch to secure.

6c

Photo 126A and 126B
Lion of Judah   1996   34" x 42"
Suzanne Muse Taylor

This striking wall hanging was inspired by the verse Revelation 5:5 in the Bible and the song, *Victory Chant*, written by Joseph Vogels © 1985. The quilt is heavily quilted and embellished with thread textured to look like the fur of a lion (detail below).

Blocking

Fabric has give and stretch in it. When a quilt is finished, it can be blocked with an iron. When I finished *Piece and Quiet* (Page 9), it rippled like crazy at the bottom where the water is. I panicked! The quilt looked great, but the waves posed a major problem. My friends helped me steam the quilt to make it lay flat, not just once, but three times. I have to laugh now when someone asks exactly how I made the water look so realistic. I tell them, "It really does wave!"

Quilt artist Libby Lehman passed this blocking tip on to me; the technique is similar to blocking needlework. Pin the quilt on the design wall. Cut a piece of muslin approximately 12" square and soak it in water. Set the iron on cotton, no steam, and spread the wet muslin over one corner of the quilt. Use the iron to press the quilt through the muslin. Continue wetting the muslin and pressing, moving across and down the quilt until the entire surface has been steamed.

Remove the muslin and use rust-resistant pins to secure the quilt to the design wall. The design wall that I use has a 2 1/2" grid. This grid can be used to square the quilt. If adjustments are required, work with the quilt when damp. Then, place rust resistant straight pins fairly close together to hold it in place (about every inch). Leave the quilt on the wall to dry. It may take a day or two.

Quilt Sleeve

The quilt is finished; it is beautiful! Now, it needs a quilt sleeve for hanging. The sleeve is a way of displaying the finished piece so that the weight is evenly distributed. It also is a way of hanging the quilt without placing holes in it. Do *not* staple a quilt to a wall. Staples eventually rust and cause damage to cloth.

It is a good idea to place a sleeve on every quilt you make, even if it is a traditional quilt that you have no intention of hanging. In the future, you or your relatives may decide to decorate a wall rather than a bed.

Make the sleeve at the same time the binding is constructed. It doesn't have to be sewn on immediately, but it will be available when you have time to put it on. If you wait until later to make the sleeve, you may not be able to find the fabric that matches the back. Or, in the interim, the fabric may accidentally be used for another project.

As in choosing quilt backings, there are decisions to consider for the sleeve. You can choose to make a sleeve from one fabric that matches the quilt backing, or the sleeve can be pieced to blend in, like the one on *Open Season,* Page 121. The same method described to make the Picture Extended Binding (Page 125), was used to create the pieced sleeve for this quilt. If the sleeve is pieced, it is a good idea to line it with another fabric in order for the hanging rod to slide through smoothly.

I use two methods of attaching a sleeve to a quilt. It depends on what the quilt is made for, and how large it is. The process of making the sleeve remains the same.

To make a quilt sleeve, measure the width of the quilt and subtract about 1 1/2". Use a rotary cutter and ruler to cut a piece of fabric about 8 1/2" wide by the sleeve length. On the short end, with the right side facing the table, fold 1/4" in from the edge, then fold again. Sew along this edge, matching the thread (Figure 127A).

Bring the two wrong sides together and stitch. Fold the sleeve in half, right sides out, and iron the seam open (Figure 127B). There is no need to have the seam on the inside of the sleeve. It will face the quilt backing and will not show. At this point you have a choice of how the sleeve is attached.

Photo 127 - *Quilter's Teddy Bear* - Detail
1999   26" x 36"   Cynthia England

Display Sleeve

This method is commonly used for quilts that are exhibited in shows that need excess fabric within the sleeve to accommodate the rods used for hanging. It is the best kind of sleeve for large quilts.

Flip the sleeve tube over, center it, and place it along the edge of the quilt back about

Figure 127A - Fold 1/4" in from the edge, and then fold again. Sew along each end.

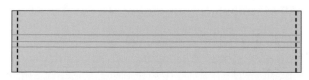

Figure 127B - Make a tube by sewing the rectangle together, right sides out.

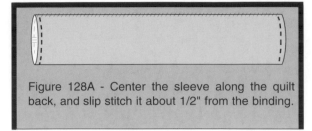

Figure 128A - Center the sleeve along the quilt back, and slip stitch it about 1/2" from the binding.

Figure 128C - Two sleeves are used to display large quilts that need a center support.

1/2" from the top of the binding (Figure 128A). Use a slip-stitch and attach the top of the sleeve to the quilt. Try to make every third stitch go through the front of the quilt, but be careful that these stitches do not show. This will make the sleeve stronger, and help to distribute the weight. After the top line of stitching is completed on the sleeve, push the quilt tube up to extend over to the bottom edge of the binding (Figure 128B). Pin it in place, and slip-stitch the bottom line of the quilt sleeve. Take a few extra stitches at the

To do this, position the sleeve along the back of the quilt before the binding is sewn on (Figure 128D). Pin it in place, and machine stitch through the sleeve at the same time the binding is stitched on. Slip-stitch the bottom of the sleeve. Keep the sleeve flat, and do not push up the sleeve when slip stitching as in the Display Sleeve method. If you do this, the top edge of the sleeve may show when the quilt hangs.

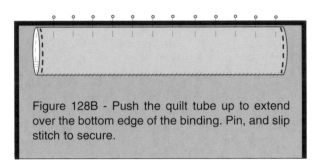

Figure 128B - Push the quilt tube up to extend over the bottom edge of the binding. Pin, and slip stitch to secure.

Figure 128D - Small light weight wall hangings can use a sleeve that is sewn into the binding.

corners for reinforcement. Pushing the edge of the sleeve up will give the rod the extra space it requires without pulling on the quilt top.

For large quilts, it is helpful to make two sleeves and leave a gap between them. Large quilts need additional hangers to sustain the weight. A nail can be placed in the wall at the gap for support (Figure 128C). Make sure the nail hits a stud.

Binding Sleeve

If the wall hanging is small (less than 30"), the top edge of the sleeve can be sewn into the binding. If you choose to do this, use a small, thin dowel or lath for hanging; an adjustable cafe curtain rod also works well. If the hanger is too thick, it will pull on the front of the quilt. This method does not allow for excess fabric to accommodate a large rod.

Photo 128 - *Lakeside Retreat* - Detail   2000
19" x 17"   Cynthia England

Labeling the Quilt

The quilt is not finished until it has a label sewn on. The label should include the maker's name, the name of the quilt, size, date completed, and the city and state. In addition, you may want to include design inspirations and any anecdotes that you would like others to know about the quilt. Imagine a relative picking up the quilt fifty years from now. What would they find interesting about the quilt or the maker?

There are many different ways to make a label. It can be written in permanent ink on muslin, embroidered, painted on, or the computer can print one for you. Test to make sure that the ink is permanent.

Use a permanent marker to make a handwritten label; make sure to heat set it when finished. To heat set, use a cotton setting, and press with an iron for a minute or so. Do *not* move the iron back and forth; moving the iron around can cause the ink to smear. Raise the iron up and down to reposition it to heat set larger labels.

Figure 129 - Line art can easily be incorporated into a computer label.

printing, remove the freezer paper, and heat set the finished label. Turn under the edges 1/4", and slip stitch to the bottom right corner of the quilt back.

Laser Printed Labels

A big advantage of computer generated labels is the ability to include as much information about the quilt as you desire, and the opportunity to add line art through the use of computer programs. Line art can be scanned and designed into the label (Figure 129).

I use my laser printer for computer-generated labels. Use a cotton setting and iron an 8 1/2" X 11" piece of freezer paper (shiny side down) to the wrong side of a piece of light colored fabric. Trim the fabric so that it is the same size as the freezer paper. Caution: Be sure that your freezer paper is entirely covered by fabric. If the waxy side of the freezer paper comes in contact with the inside of the laser printer, it can melt and cause a big mess.

Test to see which side of the paper your laser printer prints the image on. Do this by placing a mark, such as an X, on a piece of paper before running it through the printer. My printer flips the paper over as it goes through, the freezer paper side must face up for the fabric to be printed. The machine will pull the fabric through with the freezer paper attached, and this stabilizes the fabric. After

Inkjet Printed Labels

Inkjet printers can also be used to create labels. However, because inkjet inks are water-soluble, you must pre-treat the fabric or use an iron-on transfer sheet. My computer expert, Sharon Dinsmore, offers these recommendations: Iron-on transfer sheets are readily available for inkjet printers at most office supply stores and are the easiest solution for creating fabric labels with an inkjet printer. Be sure to reverse the image before printing so that when it is ironed on the fabric it will not be backwards.

If you prefer a softer hand than you can get with an iron-on transfer sheet, you'll need to purchase pre-treated fabric sheets or create your own. Be sure to purchase the washable version. To pre-treat your own fabrics, use a product called Bubble Jet Set available in many quilt stores.

Once you've treated the fabric and dried it, iron it. Make sure to get out all the wrinkles. Remove any stray fibers. Use the same steps to stabilize it with freezer paper as described for laser printers.

Remember to read and follow any manufacturer's directions when using transfer sheets.

Index

Photo 130 - *Poinsettia Basket - Detail*
1999   22" x 22"   Cynthia England

Photo 131
Cactus Country, Revisited
1998   42" X 26"   Bev Prager

This quilt is based on a black and white photograph that Bev's husband took near Texas A&M in Corpus Christi. She visited the site to observe first-hand some of the colors and other details. This is her stylized cloth version of the scene.

About the Author

Cynthia Law England is a graduate of the Art Institute of Houston, and has been creating quilts for more than twenty years. Experimentation with quilting techniques led her to develop her unique style. Straight-line stitching brought her realistic landscape images to life. She is the designer and publisher for England Design, a pattern company specializing in her Picture Piecing technique.

Cynthia's art quilts have been featured in books and numerous magazines. Her quilts have been honored with many awards, including two Best of Show awards at the prestigious International Quilt Festival. *Piece and Quiet* was distinguished as one of the 100 Best Quilts of the 20th Century. She is a native Texan and resides there with her husband, Warren, and their three children, Stephen, Travis, and Monica.

Cynthia teaches and lectures nationally and internationally. For inquiries about lecture and workshop bookings send a SASE to: Cynthia England, 1201 Sunset Drive, Dickinson, TX 77539.

Visit her website at:
www.englanddesign.com.

Resource Listing

Products:

Bernina ® of America, Inc.
3500 Thayer Court
Aurora, IL 60504-6182
(630) 978-2500
www.berninausa.com

Featherweights Fanatics ®
featherweightfanatics.com

Suncatcher Featherweights
2238 Woodwind
League City, TX 77573
(281) 332-9070
fredswitzer@worldnet.att.net

Horn Sewing Cabinets
Horn of America, Inc.
P.O. Box 608
Sutton, WV, 26601
(800) 882-8845 for nearest dealer
www.hornofamerica.com

Magic Sizing ®
Faultless Starch/Bon Ami Co.
1025 W. 8th Street
Kansas City, MO 64101-1200
www.magicsizing.com

OTT-LITE ® Technology
1214 West Cass St.
Tampa, FL 33606
(800) 842-8848
www.ott-lite.com

Reynolds ® Freezer Paper
P.O. Box 85583
Richmond, VA 23285-5583
(804) 281-4630
(800) 243-0989

Photo transfer supplies:

Bubble Jet Set ®
(888) 228-9393
www.prochemical.com

Innovative Imprints
10264 Beecher Road
Flushing, MI 48433-9728
(810) 659-6042
www.innovativeimprints.com

Batting:

Fairfield Processing Corp.
P.O. Box 1157
Danbury, CT 06813-1157
(800) 243-0989
www.poly-fil.com

Hobbs Bonded Fibers
P.O. Box 2521
Waco, TX 76702-2521
(800) 433-3357
www.hobbsbondedfibers.com

Quilters Dream Batting™
Kelsul, Inc.
3205 Foxgrove Ln.
Chesapeake, VA 23321
(888) 268-8664
www.quiltersdreambatting.com

Warm & Natural™
954 E. Union Street
Seattle, WA 98122
(800) 234-9276
www.warmcompany.com